BURIED TALENTS

OVERCOMING GENDERED SOCIALIZATION TO ANSWER GOD'S CALL

SUSAN HARRIS HOWELL

FOREWORD BY MIMI HADDAD

An imprint of InterVarsity Press
Downers Grove, Illinois

InterVarsity Press
P.O. Box 1400, Downers Grove, IL 60515-1426
ivpress.com
email@ivpress.com

InterVarsity Press® is the book-publishing division of InterVarsity Christian Fellowship/USA®, a movement of students and faculty active on campus at hundreds of universities, colleges, and schools of nursing in the United States of America, and a member movement of the International Fellowship of Evangelical Students. For information about local and regional activities, visit intervarsity.org.

Author photo by Alice Steele.

The publisher cannot verify the accuracy or functionality of website URLs used in this book beyond the date of publication.

Cover design and image composite: David Fassett
Interior design: Jeanna Wiggins
Images: young woman looking up: © Alexey_M / iStock / Getty Images Plus
colorful brushstrokes: © Asya_mix / iStock / Getty Images Plus
woman - stock illustration: © CSA Images / Getty Images
young woman, eyes closed: © Gary John Norman / The Image Bank / Getty Images
silhouette of young woman: © Glasshouse Images / The Image Bank / Getty Images
gold leaf texture: © Katsumi Murouchi / Moment / Getty Images
watercolor galaxy sky: © Khaneeros / iStock / Getty Images Plus
watercolor of galaxy: © Khaneeros / iStock / Getty Images Plus
abstract watercolor: © oxygen / Moment / Getty Images
profile of a woman looking ahead: © Tim Robberts / DigitalVision / Getty Images

ISBN 978-1-5140-0250-6 (print)
ISBN 978-1-5140-0251-3 (digital)

Printed in the United States of America ♾

InterVarsity Press is committed to ecological stewardship and to the conservation of natural resources in all our operations. This book was printed using sustainably sourced paper.

Library of Congress Cataloging-in-Publication Data
A catalog record for this book is available from the Library of Congress.

P 25 24 23 22 21 20 19 18 17 16 15 14 13 12 11 10 9 8 7 6 5 4 3 2 1
Y 37 36 35 34 33 32 31 30 29 28 27 26 25 24 23 22

To all the students of gender studies

I have taught over the years

CONTENTS

List of Tables and Figures ix

Foreword by Mimi Haddad xi

Acknowledgments xv

Introduction 1

1 Gendered Socialization in Childhood 5

2 Gendered Socialization in Adolescence 28

3 Gendered Socialization in Adulthood 45

4 Two Stories: Sarah and Michael 57

5 Creating More Accurate Self-Perceptions 69

6 Building a Support System 90

7 Paying It Forward 104

Epilogue 125

Discussion Guide 129

Resources for Women's Networking 133

Bibliography 134

LIST OF TABLES AND FIGURES

Table 1.1. Summary of childhood messages 26

Table 2.1. Erik Erikson's psychosocial stages of identity, intimacy, and generativity 36

Table 2.2. Decision making at each level of moral reasoning 43

Table 2.3. Summary of adolescent messages 44

Table 3.1. Gender differences in role expectations, communication, and gauging success 54

Figure 5.1. Interaction between affect, cognition, and overt behavior 75

FOREWORD

Mimi Haddad

In the preface to *Jane Eyre*, Charlotte Brontë (1816–1855) writes, "Conventionality is not morality. Self-righteousness is not religion. To attack the first is not to assail the last. To pluck the mask from the face of the Pharisee, is not to lift an impious hand to the Crown of Thorns."

Unmasking gendered spheres that sideline women's gifts and callings, *Buried Talents: Overcoming Gendered Socialization to Answer God's Call* is a compelling call to advance human flourishing. An astute educator and psychologist, Dr. Susan Harris Howell probes gendered socialization that confines women's contributions to gendered work with lower compensation, impoverishing whole communities. Exposing the range of macro- and microaggressions women navigate in a world that privileges males, Howell's challenge to gender essentialism—that maleness or femaleness shape identity and calling—reveals a deep distortion to Christian faith. Liberating humankind from gendered socialization, with its devaluation of women and resulting power imbalances, is nurtured by fresh reading of Scripture where the most unlikely people exercised some of the most extraordinary gifts.

This is so much the case for women that it is hard to find a single female in Scripture who did what was right while also conforming to gendered roles. Biblical leadership is first and foremost responsiveness to God. Consider two Old Testament books named after women—Esther and Ruth. We may not consider this extraordinary, yet the culture of biblical times rarely celebrated women's achievements publicly apart from the male head of their clan. To ignore gender expectations brought shame to one's family and tribe. Yet Scripture boldly honors Esther as she publicly challenges her king and husband. In shaming him, Esther obeyed God and saved Israel (Esther 4:1-17). Ruth initiated marital overtures with Boaz to save lives.

Gendered roles and identity meet a deathblow in the early chapters of Genesis. Adam's aloneness is the only "not good" in a perfect world (Genesis 2:18). In fact, Adam cannot govern the world without Eve's strength. God introduces woman as *ezer* in Hebrew, a term derived from two root words, "to be strong" and "to rescue."[1] As Eve was created from Adam's body, Adam recognizes her as "bone of my bones and flesh of my flesh" (Genesis 2:23). Scripture emphasizes not the differences between Adam and Eve, but their unity and oneness. They share a spiritual being as both are created in God's image. They also share a physical being because Eve came from Adam's body. Their shared physical and spiritual origins equip and compel a shared destiny—to work side by side caring for the earth and being fruitful (Genesis 1:27-31). Genesis 1:26 teaches that both man and woman are created in God's image to govern side by side. As God's agents, man and woman rule over the land and animals, not each other. And this, God said, is "very good" (Genesis 1:31).

Tragically, the oneness and mutuality of Eve and Adam does not endure. As man and woman rebel against God, they rupture and

[1]R. David Freedman, "Woman, a Power Equal to a Man," *Biblical Archaeology Review* 9 (1983): 1-4.

distort their relationship with God and each other. Sin's consequences include death, painful work, and male rule (Genesis 3:16-20). Profoundly, male authority serves to obscure woman's identity as bearing God's image, just as it marginalizes woman's purpose for shared work. Despite the gendered spheres resulting from male rule, women led as prophets, declaring God's truth to Israel's leaders (Exodus 15:20; 2 Chronicles 34:22). Throughout the Old Testament, women offered leadership in male-dominated fields like business (the Proverbs 31 woman), law (Deborah), and military maneuvering (Jael).

In the New Testament, Jesus was unlike the rabbis of his day. He allowed women to sit at his feet and study his teachings (Luke 10:38-42) preparing them as disciples, teachers, and evangelists. The equal dignity and purpose of women were consistently part of Christ's teachings and practices. When a woman called to Jesus saying, "Blessed is the mother who gave you birth and nursed you," Jesus responded, "Blessed rather are those who hear the word of God and obey it" (Luke 11:27-28). For Jesus, women's value resides not in their cultural roles, but in their response to God's revelation, and this becomes the standard for every member of Christ's new covenant people. Women are now daughters of Abraham (Luke 13:16), a title first used by Jesus to welcome women as heirs and full members of Christ's church.

When Christ is arrested and crucified, the Twelve apostles flee, one denies Christ openly, and others hide behind locked doors. Not the women. They understand that Christ's work is completed on a cross: a woman anoints Jesus as priests anointed the kings of Israel (Exodus 29:7; Matthew 26:6-13). Present through his crucifixion, burial, and resurrection, women were first to meet the risen Christ, and he sends them as apostles to the apostles.

Like Jesus, Paul worked beside women leaders whom he called his coworkers—women who served as evangelists, church planters, and teachers, and as a deacon and apostle. Paul summarized Christian service in Galatians 3:27-29: "As many of you as were baptized into Christ are also clothed in Christ: There is no longer Jew nor Greek, slave nor free, there is no male and female; for you are all one in Christ Jesus. And if you belong to Christ, then you are Abraham's offspring, heirs according to the promise" (NRSV). This is one of the most radical social statements ever made, particularly in Paul's culture, where identity, worth, and purpose were shaped by race, gender, and class. To this world Paul boldly declares that identity and influence are not defined by natural birth but formed through spiritual rebirth in the Spirit's power poured out on all flesh and unrestricted by gender, class, or race.

Galatians 3:27-29 does not suggest gender differences are obliterated. Paul's point is that a demeaning essentialism based on race, class, or gender dies on Calvary. In Jesus, we are a new race where the privileges of the Jew, male, and free now belong also to the Gentile, woman, and slave. Our embodied and lived gender differences comprise a rich diversity God intended for humanity and are the foundations of strength and vitality. To deprive any community, family, profession, or human endeavor of women's gifts and agency diminishes human flourishing. We can celebrate this book as it opens doors to God's gifts and calling in women for the flourishing of all. Thanks be to God.

ACKNOWLEDGMENTS

SEVERAL YEARS AGO, I told my husband I wanted to write a book. I had never written a book before and was almost afraid to say it out loud. His immediate response, "If anyone can do this, it's you," confirmed my gut feeling that this was right. Thank you, Dwayne, for having confidence in me and celebrating with me each milestone of the process.

Two wonderful friends—Dr. Deepika Reese and Alice Steele—read each chapter and provided invaluable suggestions along the way. I can't thank you two enough for your fresh eyes, honest appraisals, and confidence in me and this work.

Thank you, Melissa, for your enthusiastic encouragement and regularly reminding me that I would have all the time I needed to write this book. Hey, you were right! I did!

For providing some of the suggested exercises for creating healthier self-perceptions, my heartfelt thanks go to Chandra Heath and Brent Jones. Chandra is a licensed marriage and family therapist. Brent is not a therapist but would be phenomenal if he were! Both are former students and treasured friends.

I am indebted to two capable, meticulous, and well-organized research assistants, Hope Scott and Anna Grace Peterson. Thank you both for helping me keep my head above water during this process.

Much gratitude goes out to the professional women—in ministry, education, business, mental health, and medicine—who gave me interviews. Your stories were informative and inspirational. Thank you for sharing them with me and the readers of this book. Likewise, thanks to those who shared with me the messages they received as children. Your words gave life to the research reported here.

As a mother of grown children, I appreciate the younger parents who educated me on the books, television, and movies of children today. Thank you, Sarah Carlock, Katherine and Phillip Freeman, Keely Harris, Ashley Scott, and Dr. Abby Conway. See—those hours of watching with your children paid off!

Deja Thompson, Raegan Miller, and Dawn Richardson Starkey provided information on the language of praise music. These friends and former students are inspirational, and I appreciate their input.

My gratitude also goes to Dr. Carey Ruiz, sociologist, colleague, and friend. She answered numerous questions for me about terminology in the field. Thanks for the information and your encouragement for this book.

Many thanks go to Katelyn Howell for creating and maintaining my social media presence during the early stages of this book. And much gratitude also goes to Kelly Scott, my digital media strategist, for expanding and maintaining that presence today. I am so grateful for each of you.

My parents, Carolyn and Lowell Harris, deserve my thanks as well. They taught me to study Scripture and think for myself, and that I truly could do anything I set out to do. I love you both.

I am grateful to Campbellsville University for granting me a sabbatical so I could write. I am fortunate to work in an environment that breaks so many of the stereotypes I write about in these pages. I have always felt respected and valued there.

Many thanks go to Anna Gissing of InterVarsity Press for being enthused about this book from the start. Your suggestions helped immensely in strengthening this work.

And finally, a sincere thank you to all the gender studies students I have taught over the years. You have kept me on my toes and taught me about being a gendered individual in today's world. Thank you for giving me such hope for the future of women and men.

INTRODUCTION

A STUDENT IN MY GENDER STUDIES CLASS asked me, "If God calls women to pastor, why don't more churches have women leaders?"

Her question caught me off guard. Like many I teach, she was considering the possibility that God's call to pastor extends to women as well as men. She had listened throughout the semester as I spotlighted the many variables that influence our choices in everything from hobbies to careers. I had lectured on the power of reinforcement and punishment to shape behavior, the value of role models for skill development, and the influence of others' expectations on our self-confidence. In class, we had discussed how these processes teach us to see ourselves as capable or incapable for a variety of endeavors. We had covered how this socialization is often gender-specific and results in our feeling more suited to some occupations than others.

Yet, she didn't see the connection between years of gendered socialization and the absence of women following God's call into church leadership. Rather, she seemed to believe God's call comes to us in a vacuum, free from any misconceptions we've learned along the way—misconceptions of ourselves, what we are capable of, and where we fit into God's work. It seemed unlikely to me, however, that the processes that affect every other sphere of life would somehow stop at the church door.

I don't know how effective I was that day, some ten years ago, in broadening that student's perspective in the few remaining minutes of class. But I have tried ever since to make a more direct connection for my students between gendered socialization and the gender disparity in church leadership.

My efforts are well received. Before the semester ends (and often long after it's over), students stop by my office to relate something they heard in church or in a theology class, something that just didn't sound right. They speak up with friends and family who would limit God's work in gender-specific ways. They identify messages they've received and examine them for accuracy. Their eyes are now open, they tell me. They recognize gendered messages, confront them, and are now freer to live out God's call. Nothing could please me more.

Nothing, except taking this message to a larger audience. And herein lies the purpose of this book: to expose the subtle forms of socialization that pull women away from, and move men toward, leadership. While this book focuses on church leadership, this same socialization process also pulls women away from following God's call to lead within other sectors. This will be addressed as well.

The first three chapters explore how, from childhood through adulthood, parents, teachers, churches, the English language, and media socialize us in gender-specific ways. It examines the consequences of this socialization for our self-perceptions, relationships with others, and ultimately our call within and outside the church. Socialization, of course, varies a great deal from person to person and is dependent on many factors: the region of the country in which we grow up, early religious teachings, and the education level of our parents, to name a few. For this reason, readers will vary in terms of their awareness of and exposure to the socialization described in these pages.

Chapter four illustrates how years of gendered socialization culminate in the choices of one man and one woman. It shows how those choices result in different outcomes for these two fictional, yet all-too-real individuals, outcomes often accepted as the inevitable result of sex differences rather than the result of socialization.

The last three chapters will help you assess the accuracy of messages you have received, create more accurate self-perceptions, and build a support system that will encourage you to follow your call. This section will also help solidify what you have learned by encouraging you to pay it forward to future generations of girls and women.

One book cannot cover every aspect of a topic as broad as gender. For instance, *intersectionality*—the study of how gender, race, and class intersect to create distinctive forms of discrimination—is undeniably important. Considering gender apart from these other factors may not capture the whole experience. However, examining gender socialization and the impact it has on vocation remains a worthy and practical goal. This book focuses on one important "piece of the puzzle" with the understanding that other books will also be needed. Though gender socialization is certainly also relevant to discussions of transgender and nonbinary experiences, there is, unfortunately, not space in this book to tease out the implications for these readers.

If you are a woman who has buried her talent to lead, this book will show how your perceptions were shaped and how that has affected your work for God's kingdom, both inside and outside of the church. You will find ways to overcome these obstacles in your own life and help others do the same.

If you are a student in theology or the social sciences, this book will show how the process of socialization affects women and men differently. You will learn how to make a difference for those within your personal, ministerial, or professional spheres of influence.

1 GENDERED SOCIALIZATION IN CHILDHOOD

THIS CHAPTER EXPLORES gendered socialization in childhood and its impact on achievement motivation. Preschool children are socialized primarily through family members and those over whom caregivers have some control. As children enter school, however, their world broadens to include teachers, coaches, and a larger pool from which they can choose friends. These children are now influenced by people their primary caregivers don't know as well, and systems (e.g., the school and religious community) over which they have less control. In addition, greater access to television, movies, and books supply these children with gendered expectations from an increasingly larger community.

In this chapter, we will examine the messages these preschool and elementary school children are given through toys selected for them, a gendered division of labor, the education system, the English language, and media (books, television, and movies) regarding their place in the world as boys and girls. We will explore how this socialization impacts their occupational goals and the likelihood they will achieve those goals.

TOY SELECTION

One trip down the aisle of any toy store will convince even the casual observer that boys and girls are encouraged to play with different toys.[1] However, before children are old enough to choose the pink package with the girl on the front or the blue one with the boy, the choices are made for them. Parents and others bearing gifts supply boys with cars and trucks, sports paraphernalia, and tool sets, and they provide girls with dolls, kitchen sets, and toy appliances. If children are less than enthused, someone will encourage her to "rock the baby" or him to "throw the ball."

Preschool boys are often given leeway in picking up the occasional doll or pretending to fix dinner. However, they often age out of this luxury within a few short years. Not long after entering school, they will encounter subtle reprimands and even ridicule for playing with a toy vacuum cleaner or dish set. Girls, however, are given more than leeway; their parents often show pride when they pick up a ball and bat. I've taught many women who boasted of their tomboy days. Any men labeled as sissies haven't announced it in my classes.[2]

Of course, when children begin playing with other boys and girls, they quickly learn which toys are considered appropriate for their own sex and specifically ask for them. The first time our daughter attended a friend's birthday party, she came home excited about all the Barbie dolls her friend had received and told me the ones she wanted for her own birthday. We entered a new era that day. She would no longer blindly accept the toys we selected for her. From

---

[1]For an examination of the debate surrounding gendered toy marketing, see Cordelia Fine and Emma Rush, "'Why Does All the Girls Have to Buy Pink Stuff?' The Ethics and Science of the Gendered Toy Marketing Debate," *Journal of Business Ethics* 149 (2018).

[2]For an examination of age as a variable in gendered toy preferences, see Brenda K. Todd et al., "Sex Differences in Children's Toy Preferences: A Systematic Review, Meta-Regression, and Meta-Analysis," *Infant and Child Development* 27, no. 2 (2018).

here on, we would work harder to balance out the pink-aisle toys that are the staple of girls' birthday parties.

Students ask me, "What's wrong with any of these toys?" Nothing, I tell them. We gave our daughter a kitchen set *and* a tool set. We gave our son Matchbox cars *and* dolls. My husband and I made a variety of toys available and tried not to push one kind on our daughter and another on our son. It's the restrictiveness, I tell them, that creates the problem.

When the little boy is consistently shamed for picking up a doll or his attention diverted when he pretends to fix dinner, he learns that housework and childcare are women's work. With this message confirmed in everything from commercials to magazine covers, is it any wonder that as a new father he's uncomfortable caring for his own infant? Fearful of holding her, lest she break? He doesn't have the mindset nor the experience to feel comfortable as caregiver to a newborn.

The girl, however, learns that housework and childcare *are* for her and, what's more, are unacceptable for boys. Her mindset tells her, *Boys shouldn't take care of children. They don't know how. I should; I'm better at it.* And in fact, she *will* get better at it than the boys she knows. She will learn what to do with babies: the soft voice to use when they cry, and the way to hold them, give them a bottle, or rock them to sleep.

Now, imagine her as an adult. She and hubby have their first baby. Daddy picks up the newborn for the first time and is scared and clueless. *Why is he crying?! I don't know what I'm doing!* It's easy for him to assume: *Caring for young children is not for me!* Handing the baby to Mommy seems the humane thing to do. While she is likely just as scared—because her childhood dolls didn't cry as often or relentlessly as this tiny human!—her mindset tells her, *I better figure this out. I'm the Mommy.*

So, she does.

And he does not.

The next time baby cries, who picks him up? Probably the one who had more success last time. The Mommy. And after a while, it becomes easier and easier for her because she's getting practice, learning what does and doesn't work. Meanwhile, he's in awe of how she *just knows* what to do! Must be instinct, he says. God's design. He will read somewhere that the best thing he can do for his children is to love their mother, so he goes back to work and tries to stay out of the way. And with that, his status is reduced to auxiliary parent. Support staff.

No surprise then that she's reluctant to leave the baby with Daddy. When she tells her friends that he's watching the little guy, she says it with an eye roll and a playful gritting of the teeth. What she'll find when she gets home is anybody's guess. She better not be gone long!

What is taken as instinct is more likely her having learned childcare skills through countless opportunities to practice them beginning the moment she was given her first doll. And more important, she was given the message early on that childcare was something she could and *should* do. It was her job.

But it doesn't stop there. Believing she is naturally better at meeting her child's needs, she might find it difficult to release infant care to another capable person when she goes back to work. It feels unnatural, a disservice to her child. So, she might do what many others do: switch to part-time work or give up working outside the home entirely while her baby is little. However, removing herself from the workforce will slow her career progression if not derail it entirely. Even the part-time alternative narrows her options, typically to jobs with less responsibility, lower status, reduced pay, and fewer chances for promotion.

Understand that I'm not calling for children to take a backseat to career advancement. Parenting is arguably one of the most important tasks we can take on. In fact, women are told that raising children is far more important than any job, or even *ministry*, they could otherwise pursue. Yet, if it were that simple, couples everywhere would *vie* for who gets to stay home with children. But they don't. In fact, fathers are virtually never told to sideline their work in favor of the more important role as their child's primary caregiver. Why not? Because for men to do so would risk their occupational future and the opportunities that entails.

I've taught this enough to know that this is where a student will remind me that we are all called to serve and to raise good children. Why are women balking at doing something God has called us all to do? To that I say, precisely—we are *all* called to serve, and if we have children, we are called to raise them well. These aren't jobs just assigned to women. Rather, I contend that mothers carry the lion's share of childcare responsibilities because of an inaccurate belief that they are naturally better at it, and that men can't, or shouldn't, learn those skills.

This mindset has far-reaching consequences for the time a mother can devote to ministry or any occupation to which she is called. Doors will close for her that remain open for the father of the same child.

DIVISION OF LABOR

Children observe and often take part in the division of labor at home. Even with more women in the workforce than in previous generations, women still do most of the household work with the same gender differences reflected in children's chore assignments.[3] Children typically see men perform outdoor tasks, such as lawn care

[3]For information on women and housework, see Mylene Lachance-Grzela and Genevieve Bouchard, "Why Do Women Do the Lion's Share Of Housework? A Decade of Research," *Sex Roles* 63 (2010): 777, https://doi.org/10.1007/s11199-010-9797-z. For information on children's

and building repair, along with indoor maintenance, such as painting or appliance maintenance. They see women care for children and complete indoor chores, such as cleaning, laundry, and food preparation. In this division of labor, women and girls complete tasks that need to be done regularly, sometimes daily. Men and boys do tasks that need to be done sporadically. Grass isn't cut as often as food is prepared or dishes washed. Rooms aren't painted as frequently as clothes are laundered.

A newlywed student told me she and her husband agreed to a similar arrangement before they married. But before long she noticed that her after-work hours were spent cooking, doing laundry, and cleaning while her husband sat in the recliner watching TV. Evidently, he was paying a teenager to mow the grass once a week during warm weather. Until snow fell on the driveway or leaves from the trees, he had completed his share of household responsibilities. They could afford it and, as he reminded her, she had agreed to the arrangement. However, they could not afford to hire someone to do all her chores, nor did he offer to pick up any of them to create a more equitable arrangement. This division of labor results in more work for women and girls, less for men and boys.

What will Dad do with his extra time? He will probably devote it to a job that keeps him away from home for a major portion of each day. He won't need to leave work early to shop for groceries and make dinner, do laundry, or provide homework assistance. Likewise, the son will consider a wide range of career options since even the most time consuming and educationally intensive will not pose an obstacle to his having a family of his own one day. (Incidentally, these careers will probably pay more, too.) He will assume, as will his employer, that someone else will be the primary caregiver

---

chore assignments, see Sara Raley and Suzanne Bianchi, "Sons, Daughters, and Family Processes: Does Gender of Children Matter?," *Annual Review of Sociology* 32 (2006): 401.

for his young children and at home when the older ones return from school.

This *second shift*[4] of work awaiting Mother at home often limits the amount of time she will devote to an occupation. When asked to work late or apply for a promotion, she will question the wisdom of being away from home for long periods of time. Who will take the older child to the dentist then soccer practice or make sure the younger one starts on that science project right after piano lessons? Or maybe she won't be asked to work late at all or even considered for a promotion since she has likely voiced to her coworkers and boss the precarious balance she maintains between work and home. When the daughter considers career options, her plans are likely to be as grand as her brother's. At first. The older she gets, however, the more she will consider how many children she wants, and from watching all her mother does, she will tone down her aspirations.

Indeed, daughters of fathers who do more domestic tasks have career aspirations that are less stereotypical than those who do not.[5] Alyssa Croft and colleagues suggest that these girls might be learning to expect the same from a future partner, freeing them to consider occupations that require more of their time.[6] Likewise, fathers who do not contribute as much to housework and childcare might implicitly communicate a different set of expectations.

One study of eighteen-year-old women who aspired to male-dominated careers found that by the age of twenty-five, 82 percent of them had changed to careers that were either gender-neutral or

---

[4]The phrase "second shift" was coined by Arlie Hochschild with Anne Machung in the book *The Second Shift: Working Families and the Revolution at Home* (New York: Penguin, 1989). For more information on the second shift today, see Mary Blair-Loy et al., "Stability and Transformation in Gender, Work, and Family: Insights from *The Second Shift* for the Next Quarter Century," *Community, Work, and Family* 18, no. 4 (2015): 435-54.

[5]Alyssa Croft et al., "The Second Shift Reflected in the Second Generation: Do Parents' Gender Roles at Home Predict Children's Aspirations?," *Psychological Science* 25, no. 7 (2014): 1418.

[6]Croft et al., "Second Shift Reflected," 1426.

female-dominated.[7] The best predictor for the change in career aspirations was their desire for a family-flexible job.[8] Another study of high-achieving girls ages fifteen to seventeen found that they were less likely to plan for a career when they also planned to have children. They anticipated social pressure to give up work or scale it down to care for their children, and it was already shaping their educational and career plans.[9] Likewise, another study found young adult women moving toward more traditional, less prestigious careers than they had planned their last year of high school, toward careers that "underutilized their abilities."[10] These findings were illustrated for me recently when a young woman shared that her childhood occupational goals, alongside teaching and motherhood, included being "wife to the president of the United States." Evidently, being president herself was out of the question.

Is it any surprise that when this girl becomes a woman with her own family, her career and ministry goals will take second place to her husband's? It will be a tacit understanding. They won't say it in so many words. Not to each other, not even to themselves. It will just feel *right* somehow. Neither of them will think about how the messages they received shaped their thinking about something as sacred as their work for God.

And speaking of work for God, children who attend church typically witness a division of labor that fits into the parameters they've seen at home. Men serve as leaders. They are pastors, deacons, elders, and music directors. They lead classes for men or ones with both

---

[7]Pamela M. Frome et al., "Why Don't They Want a Male-Dominated Job? An Investigation of Young Women Who Changed Their Occupational Aspirations," *Educational Research and Evaluation* 12, no. 4 (2006): 359.

[8]Frome et al., "Why Don't They Want a Male-Dominated Job?," 359.

[9]Gillian Marks and Diane M. Houston, "The Determinants of Young Women's Intentions About Education, Career Development and Family Life," *Journal of Education and Work* 15, no. 3 (2002): 321.

[10]Karen M. O'Brien et al., "Attachment, Separation, and Women's Vocational Development: A Longitudinal Analysis," *Journal of Counseling Psychology* 47, no. 3 (2000): 311.

men and women. Women serve as support. They are church secretaries, fellowship coordinators, and nursery workers. When they lead, they serve as children or youth ministers, teach classes for women, or lead mission organizations. Occasionally, women serve as associate pastors, but often under a man who is identified as the senior pastor. Such a distinction confirms the message children frequently receive at home: women manage children and provide support for men who lead.

Granted, what I describe is not the reality for every man or woman, boy or girl. Fewer families today hold to the traditional roles that have almost dictated occupational choices for previous generations. Yet, as a professor and mentor of young adults, I can attest to this pattern being alive and well among college students today. Young women often bring up their desire for marriage and children as a consideration in whether they will pursue graduate school and careers that require extensive time commitments. While the young men who come to me for career guidance have their share of concerns, I have never in over two decades had one of them tell me they were unsure about whether to pursue their call given their desire to get married and have children.

Never.

Not one.

EDUCATION

Imagine you are a child who brings home an A on a math test. Your parents say, "That's great! You're really smart!" Or they say, "That's great! You worked really hard!" Both responses are positive, right? Each communicates congratulations and pride. Yet these two comments differ in ways that are important for achievement motivation.

The first comment communicates that the A in math was earned due to a stable attribute—being smart, something that's part of who you are and is therefore likely to be repeated. After all, if you're smart today, you'll still be smart next week, next month, next year, and so on.

The second comment suggests that the A is due to an unstable attribute—hard work, something that is situational and therefore could easily change with the next assignment or task. What if you don't have as much time to study the next time or what if the material is just harder and your effort isn't enough?

Of course, either comment might be appropriate at different times with different children. Yet when children succeed in math, parents more often credit their son's success to talent, their daughter's to effort,[11] implying that his success in this "masculine" subject will be repeated, but that hers is more tenuous. As Hannu Raty and colleagues state, "In both mathematics and reading, girls were not entitled to ability-based attribution to the same extent as were boys."[12]

To be fair, parents' beliefs might be a holdover from past decades when, on average, boys *did* outscore girls in math, leading many to assume boys had more natural talent in this subject than girls. But recently, this difference is mainly limited to countries where girls receive fewer educational opportunities and where women hold fewer jobs in research.[13] In fact, some claim that in

---

[11]Hannu Raty et al., "Parents' Explanations of Their Child's Performance in Mathematics and Reading: A Replication and Extension of Yee and Eccles," *Sex Roles* 46, no. 3/4 (2002): 121.

[12]Raty et al., "Parents' Explanations of Their Child's Performance," 121. Findings from this research should not be taken to diminish the value of hard work in academic achievement. In fact, research reveals that a growth mindset, which conceptualizes intelligence as something one can develop rather than existing as a fixed trait, is associated with higher levels of academic achievement. See Susana Claro, David Paunesku, and Carol S. Dweck, "Growth Mindset Tempers the Effects of Poverty on Academic Achievement," *Proceedings of the National Academy of Sciences of the United States of America* 113, no. 31 (2016): 8664. There appears to be a difference in communicating to someone that their success is due to hard work *rather than* ability and communicating that intelligence can be developed with effort.

[13]Nicole M. Else-Quest, Janet Shibley Hyde, and Marcia C. Linn, "Cross-national Patterns of Gender Differences in Mathematics: A Meta-Analysis," *Psychological Bulletin* 136, no. 1 (2010): 103.

the United States, gender differences no longer exist.[14] What was considered an innate difference is likely a difference in the expectations, opportunities, and encouragement boys and girls receive for mathematical accomplishment.

This hasn't become common knowledge, however, as many teachers and parents still believe boys are more capable in math, and boys tend to show more confidence and less anxiety than girls do in this subject.[15] Such was the case for a woman who recently shared her experience with me. Counselors pushed what they saw as her natural talent in English even though she also made good grades in math and science. However, instead of attributing her grades in these subjects to talent, she was given the message that math and science were difficult subjects and was discouraged from pursuing either.

But does it matter? Won't their scores convince these girls that they aren't mathematically deficient?

Evidently not. Teacher bias has been found to have a detrimental effect on math and science achievement in girls.[16] Lavy and Sand conclude that such an effect during these early years serves to discourage girls' participation in advanced math in high school, which in turn preempts their pursuing careers in which math is foundational.[17]

---

[14]Janet S. Hyde et al., "Gender Similarities Characterize Math Performance," *Science* 321, no. 5888 (2008): 495.

[15]For information on teachers' beliefs, see Joseph P. Robinson-Cimpian et al., "Teachers' Perceptions of Students' Mathematics Proficiency May Exacerbate Early Gender Gaps in Achievement," *Developmental Psychology* 50, no. 4 (2014): 1279. For information on parents' beliefs, see Jennifer Herbert and Deborah Stipek, "The Emergence of Gender Differences in Children's Perceptions of Their Academic Competence," *Journal of Applied Developmental Psychology* 26 (2005): 276. For information on boys' confidence, see Herbert and Stipek, "Emergence of Gender Differences," 290. For information on girls' anxiety, see Else-Quest et al., "Cross-national Patterns of Gender Differences in Mathematics," 122.

[16]For information on the effect of teacher bias, see Victor Lavy and Edith Sand, "On the Origins of Gender Gaps in Human Capital: Short- and Long-Term Consequences of Teachers' Biases," *Journal of Public Economics* 167 (2018): 263, and Michela Carlana, "Implicit Stereotypes: Evidence from Teachers' Gender Bias," *The Quarterly Journal of Economics* 134, no. 3 (2019): 1219.

[17]Lavy and Sand, "On the Origins of Gender Gaps," 263.

In fact, among eight- and nine-year-old girls, self-confidence in math is driven less by grades and more by their perceptions of teacher evaluation.[18] This suggests that when a girl performs as well as the boys, she will pay less attention to her grade and more to teacher comments, which, given the stereotype, will downplay her natural ability. The boy's confidence, however, is based on a combination of grades and perceived teacher evaluation,[19] which—again, that stereotype—attributes his grades to natural ability. This fosters different levels of self-confidence in children who are equally gifted in the same subject. And self-confidence is important if girls are to persist in math and other areas seen as masculine, such as science and engineering.[20] In fact, confidence is so important in these areas that Mau concludes, "Parents, teachers, and counselors must be aware of how their expectations and attitudes affect the math and science achievement of their students and, in turn, affect their students' vocational interests."[21]

I don't suggest that parents and teachers intentionally foster self-confidence in boys while undermining the same in girls. Yet subtle messages communicate expectations that parents and teachers themselves might not even realize they hold.

For instance, when asked which courses they wanted their children to take in high school, mothers of sons more often than

---

[18]Oliver Dickhauser and Wulf-Uwe Meyer, "Gender Differences in Young Children's Math Ability Attributions," *Psychology Science* 48, no. 1 (2006): 12.

[19]Dickhauser and Meyer, "Gender Differences in Young Children's Math," 12.

[20]For information on the importance of self-confidence in math, see Gail Crombie et al., "Predictors of Young Adolescents' Math Grades and Course Enrollment Intentions: Gender Similarities and Differences," *Sex Roles* 52, no. 5/6 (2005): 364. For information on the importance of self-confidence in science and engineering, see Wei-Cheng Mau, "Factors that Influence Persistence in Science and Engineering Career Aspirations," *The Career Development Quarterly* 51 (2003): 241, and Carol A. Heaverlo, Robyn Cooper, and Frankie Santos Lannan, "STEM Development: Predictors for 6th-12th Grade Girls' Interest and Confidence in Science and Math," *Journal of Women and Minorities in Science and Engineering* 19, no. 2 (2013): 121-42.

[21]Mau, "Factors That Influence Persistence," 241.

mothers of daughters selected science.[22] Why? They claimed science lacked usefulness for their daughters who were not as good in this subject.[23] As one mother stated: "I didn't put any kind of science because she's not good at science so I don't think she'd grasp it later on."[24] This, despite the lack of gender differences in science grades.[25] Another study found parents giving three times the explanations to their sons than to their daughters about science exhibits in a museum.[26] Given the stereotype of boys' natural talent in "masculine" subjects, parents might believe their investment in boys' learning will provide a greater payoff.

But wait. Does any of this have long-term consequences? Some say it does not. Women are slightly more likely than men to attend college, a fact sometimes touted as proof that inequality has all but ceased.[27]

However, the academic choices of these students say otherwise. Men are still more likely to graduate with degrees in computer science, engineering, math, the physical sciences, theology and religious studies; women, more often in the biological sciences, family and consumer sciences, and education.[28] And among women who

---

[22]Harriet R. Tenenbaum and Dionna May, "Gender in Parent-Child Relationships," in *Gender and Development*, ed. Patrick J. Leman and Harriet R. Tenenbaum (London: Psychology Press, 2014), 6.

[23]Tenenbaum and May, "Gender in Parent-Child Relationships," 5-6.

[24]Tenenbaum and May, "Gender in Parent-Child Relationships," 6.

[25]Tenenbaum and May, "Gender in Parent-Child Relationships," 5.

[26]Kevin Crowley et al., "Parents Explain More Often to Boys Than to Girls During Shared Scientific Thinking," *Psychological Science* 12, no. 3 (2001): 258.

[27]Digest of Education Statistics, "Recent High School Completers and Their Enrollment in College, by Sex and Level of Institution: 1960-2019," National Center for Education Statistics, https://nces.ed.gov/programs/digest/d20/tables/dt20_302.10.asp.

[28]For information on degrees conferred to males, see Digest of Education Statistics, "Bachelor's Degrees Conferred to Males by Postsecondary Institutions, by Race/Ethnicity and Field of Study: 2017-2018 and 2018-2019," National Center for Education Statistics, https://nces.ed.gov/programs/digest/d20/tables/dt20_322.40.asp. For information on degrees conferred to females, see Digest of Education Statistics, "Bachelor's Degrees Conferred to Females by Postsecondary Institutions, by Race/Ethnicity and Field of Study: 2017-2018 and 2018-2019," National Center for Education Statistics, https://nces.ed.gov/programs/digest/d20/tables/dt20_322.50.asp.

do enter STEM (science, technology, engineering, math) careers, after twelve years, half of them switch to non-STEM occupations.[29] The choice of college majors and career aspirations falls along stereotyped lines and is consistent with the gendered messages these individuals have likely received throughout their lives.

Textbooks add another layer to the messages these children receive, namely, that women do not achieve in ways that matter. School books follow the history of men (*White* men, at that) and confine the experiences of women to a few in-text references, sidebars, or chapters on women's issues. One study of twelve introductory American government and politics textbooks found "9% of pages included in-text references to women, 28% of images and 17% of sidebars, tables, figures, and charts included women."[30] Role models for female achievement are scarce. The struggles for equal pay and women's suffrage and against sexual harassment in the workplace are presented as peripheral issues outside the main. Men are the norm; women, the exception. Men accomplish in ways that are notable; women, not so much.

What can we learn here? The stereotype of gender differences in natural ability in math and science persists despite evidence to the contrary. Boys are often told in subtle ways that success in these areas reflects their essence and will continue; girls, that theirs is due to effort and is, therefore, less certain. Girls often receive less attention and instruction even though their success equals that of boys. Since girls' self-confidence is buoyed by feedback, the relative absence of it diminishes their self-perception as talented in these "masculine" subjects and decreases the likelihood they will continue in them. Textbooks confirm that women rarely rank among the achievers.

---

[29]Jennifer L. Glass et al., "What's So Special About STEM: A Comparison of Women's Retention in STEM and Professional Occupations," *Social Forces* 92, no. 2 (2013): 734.

[30]Christiane Olivo, "Bringing Women In: Gender and American Government and Politics in Textbooks," *Journal of Political Science Education* 8 (2012): 131.

And what does this suggest about a woman's motivation to achieve in other areas overwhelmingly dominated by men—church leadership, for example? If the research cited here is any indication, she will believe she is less qualified than men for these jobs. And she will feel this way even when she is successful and receives objective evidence of that success. Like the girl whose grades are equal to the boys', the woman pastor will focus less on indicators of her successful ministry and more on the comments made by others that downplay her natural ability in this male domain. And like the girl whose diminished self-confidence discourages her continuing in math, the woman minister with lower self-confidence will not likely stay in ministry, at least not in a leadership position.

I don't suggest that teachers, parents, or textbook authors set out to hold girls and women back. I am convinced that it is unintentional and that most would be surprised to learn that they fall into the patterns described here. Rather, all of us—caregivers and educators included—are often blind to the ways our culture shapes us and how we perpetuate the same with those in our care. This isn't about blame. Instead, I suggest that knowing what shapes our beliefs about ourselves and how those beliefs inform our decisions is the first step to a more accurate mindset and more informed decisions.

THE ENGLISH LANGUAGE

Language provides another avenue through which children learn their place in society as males and females. The English language is androcentric, meaning it is male-oriented. It communicates that women play a peripheral or secondary role to the main players, who are men.

Until recently, it was considered proper to use the masculine generic for any person within a group composed of both sexes (e.g., "Each student will buy his own lunch"). A singular, gender-neutral word to represent us all simply did not exist in the English language, we were told. Besides, since women and girls know they are included, there isn't a problem, is there?

Women would argue that there are several problems: lack of clarity, for one. Consider the phrase "every man shall receive his own reward according to his own labour" (1 Corinthians 3:8 KJV). In that context, do *man* and *his* mean all humans or specifically men as opposed to women? Also, the masculine generic treats women as an afterthought. One could hardly blame the girl for feeling like an afterthought when that verse is read in Sunday school and her teacher explains, "Of course, that means you too."

Then came the cumbersome *his or her*, as in "Each student will buy his or her own lunch." "Each student will buy his/her own lunch" was still a bit gangly. And perhaps my least favorite, "(S)he will need to buy lunch." Talk about feeling like an afterthought.

Recently, it's become acceptable to use the plural pronoun *they* when referring to someone not identified specifically as male or female. Although some purists balk at the use of a plural pronoun to identify an individual, I appreciate the effort to make our language more inclusive. In his article with a tongue-in-cheek title, "Everyone Uses Singular 'They,' Whether They Realize It or Not," Geoff Nunberg reminds us that *they* already has a long history of common usage as a singular pronoun.[31] Likewise, we now hear *chairperson* instead of *chairman* and *firefighter* in place of *fireman*, indicating that our language is evolving.

Changes are slow in coming, however. Several years ago, my Sunday school class asked for volunteers to *man* the church's booth at a local festival. I commented on the term and received a chuckle

[31]Geoff Nunberg, "Everyone Uses Singular 'They,' Whether They Realize It or Not," *Fresh Air*, NPR, January 13, 2016, www.npr.org/2016/01/13/462906419/everyone-uses-singular-they-whether-they-realize-it-or-not.

from someone who asked if I would prefer to *woman* the booth. Evidently that sounded silly. Aside from the fact that for me to *man* the booth also sounded silly, the term was inaccurate since half of those involved would be women. When I suggested we *work* the booth, however, the class agreed.

My students also find it difficult at times to come up with gender-neutral terms for common phrases. I ask them to find inclusive terminology for words such as *mastermind* or phrases like *Be a man!* They typically laugh as they suggest *mistressmind* and acknowledge that *Be a woman!* doesn't have the same meaning at all. Of course, it doesn't.

So, I urge them to consider what the terms are intended to communicate. A mastermind denotes the brains behind an event, someone who orchestrates something complex. So why imply, through the use of the masculine *master*, that men are the only ones capable of orchestrating something complex? *Be a man!* is another way to say *Be an adult!* So why not just say that? It's more accurate and doesn't restrict adulthood to men.

But the androcentricity of language goes beyond the masculine generic. Women almost always take their husbands' surnames at marriage. A 2004 survey of Americans found only 6 percent of married women had a nonconventional surname—that is, they retained their own surname, hyphenated, or used two surnames.[32] And although the usage of *Mr. Man's Name and Mrs. Woman's Name* is becoming more common, it is still deemed appropriate to refer to a married couple as *Mr. and Mrs. Man's Name*, leaving her name out entirely. Before the title *Ms.* came into usage in the 1970s, single women were identified as *Miss* and married women as *Mrs.*—many still are—while men have always been referred to as *Mr.* regardless

[32]Gretchen E. Gooding and Rose M. Kreider, "Women's Marital Naming Choices in a Nationally Representative Sample," *Journal of Family Issues* 31, no. 5 (2010): 681.

of marital status. The implication is that her identity, but not his, is tied to having a spouse. The use of *Ms.* therefore is to "give women a title that makes their autonomy central, not to highlight their relationship or absence of a relationship, to a man."[33]

Likewise, when a role or an occupation is filled by a woman, the suffix *-ess* or *-ette* is often attached. Female actors and waiters are commonly referred to as actresses and waitresses; an unmarried woman, a bachelorette. The very notion that a title be reduced to its diminutive form when held by a woman is inherently demeaning. Her work, although identical to a man's, is not worthy of the same respect. Similarly, calling a woman a *girl* reduces her status to that of a child; using it as an insult (e.g., "He runs like a girl") is—well—insulting.

Male-centered language also sets the framework for our relationship with God and the roles we play within the church when we hear and sing those words and phrases repeatedly. Although less common in contemporary worship music, traditional hymns often exclude the female experience, implying that God's work is done *through* men and *for* men. "Faith of Our Fathers" (1849) mentions the persecution men have endured. In "Rise Up, O Men of God" (1911), we are encouraged to "bring in the brotherhood." "Hark! The Herald Angels Sing" (1739) reminds us that Christ was "born that man no more may die" and "to raise the sons of earth."

Occasionally, I've been admonished not to be "so picky." I've received a few eye rolls when I've pointed out that our language excludes and demeans women. So, I ask my students to imagine the situation in reverse, that our language was so heavily oriented toward women that men regularly felt excluded. For instance, what if we

[33]Eve Kay, "Call Me Ms," *The Guardian*, June 29, 2007, www.theguardian.com/world/2007/jun/29/gender.uk?fbclid=IwAR0dclIGUIeLvUDd7oYclf-Nzv0nyMYN1tvAV-aQXbRGlXELyazjcmriI7w.

referred to all people as *she* or *her* and expected boys and men to just know they're included? What if we communicated that only women filled jobs that men also filled on a regular basis? What if we expected new husbands to take their wives' surnames and expected them to be okay with mail addressed to *Mrs. and Mr. Woman's Name*? What if we attached a diminutive suffix to a word when it denoted a man? What if we referred to older gentlemen as *boys* or hurled the word at women as an insult when they didn't perform well? What if worship music spoke readily about the sisterhood and women of faith but seldom about the brotherhood and men of God?

Would it still seem picky?

Of course not. I would expect men to be upset and demand changes in the way we speak about them. Because regardless of our intent, language communicates what we believe and constructs a framework through which the next generation of women and men will build their own beliefs. Language is one vehicle through which we learn to see ourselves in relation to others and in relation to God.

MEDIA (BOOKS, TELEVISION, AND MOVIES)

Those who would influence our perception of products and increase our willingness to buy them often use television to do so. Ratings on movies and music attest to the widespread belief that these forms of media influence children in ways that concern their caregivers. While most concern centers on aggressive and sexual content, harmful gender stereotypes are often overlooked, especially when embedded in beloved classics touted as family friendly. Concern is warranted, however, given the association between viewing gender stereotypes in media and children holding stereotyped attitudes.[34]

[34]Patrice Oppliger, "Effects of Gender Stereotyping on Socialization," in *Mass Media Effects Research: Advances Through Meta-Analysis*, ed. Raymond W. Preiss et al. (Mahwah, NJ: Lawrence Erlbaum Associates, 2007), 208, 210.

Likewise, viewing reality dating programs (RDP) is related to college students' "endorsement of gender stereotypical attitudes toward and beliefs about dating and relationships."[35] My students tell me no harm results since they know reality shows are no more real than the fairy tales they watched as children. But according to the RDP study, it doesn't matter. The relationship holds regardless of whether students are watching to learn or merely for entertainment.[36]

Thankfully, the past few decades have delivered a more balanced portrayal of females in children's literature and programming. In the 1990s, children were introduced to J. K. Rowling's Harry Potter series and Craig McCracken's Powerpuff Girls. The first decade of the 2000s gave us Dora the Explorer and The Hunger Games, with the Divergent series following soon after. In the past decade, Moana, Doc McStuffins, Dino Dana, and Lucky from the Spirit series provided even more strong female characters to entertain and inspire this generation of children. (I was surprised to hear one young man tell that as a child in the 1990s he was not permitted to even watch programs featuring a female protagonist or one who was Black.)

Yet these characters were not standard fare during the childhoods of most women today. Rather, the classics, replete with gender stereotypes, provided much of the material read to us as children and later served up through movies and television programs. And while current trends present a more robust image of females, the classics will likely continue to engage readers and viewers for generations to come since they are, well, classics.

In these stories, the woman is vulnerable, helpless, and in need of a prince to kiss her awake, rescue her from the evil witch, or retrieve the slipper she lost the night before. Rarely do women in these

[35]Eileen L. Zurbriggen and Elizabeth M. Morgan, "Who Wants to Marry a Millionaire? Reality Dating Television Programs, Attitudes Toward Sex, and Sexual Behaviors," *Sex Roles* 54, no. 1/2 (2006): 11.

[36]Zurbriggen and Morgan, "Who Wants to Marry a Millionaire?," 13.

stories rescue men from misfortune. And despite their gaining security through a man's favor, they don't *do* much to gain that favor. Other than being beautiful, of course. And kind. They must be kind. This presents girls with substantially fewer role models for accomplishment and, in fact, communicates that her job is to be attractive so someone *else* will get her what she wants.

The message for boys in these classics is also problematic: they win the lady fair through derring-do, then hold on to her by showering her with gifts. So, besides the physique and bravery required to slay dragons, he must be wealthy too. Even so, children's self-esteem increases more when they hear stories with role models of their own sex.[37] Girls are, therefore, at a disadvantage when characters they most identity with accomplish little and depend on the opposite sex to meet their needs.

When I speak on this topic, I'm frequently asked if I read fairy tales to my children and if they watched movies or television at all. I respond that, yes, my children knew about Cinderella and Snow White and watched their share of movies and TV. However, my husband and I exposed them to a variety of each with strong girls and women in the mix. (I also took a few liberties here and there when I read to them. In my version, for instance, Cinderella married the prince, went to medical school, and only then did they live happily ever after.)

I must confess, however, that I question the wisdom of exposing children to these stories at all. I would never read a story to any child that depicted one race as vulnerable, helpless, and needy while touting the other as brave, accomplished, and heroic. I just wouldn't. It would teach them an ideology I find deplorable. Yet most of us do not notice, much less feel outrage, when children hear, read, and

[37]Jan M. Ochman, "The Effects of Nongender-Role Stereotyped, Same-Sex Role Models in Storybooks on the Self-Esteem of Children in Grade Three," *Sex Roles* 35, no. 11-12 (1996): 711.

watch story after story in which women are depicted as helpless while men are depicted as their heroes.

In summary, children receive a host of gendered messages from family, the church, the education system, the English language, and media sources that channel their focus toward some pursuits and away from others (see table 1.1). These messages are subtle yet exert a powerful influence on the girl and boy as they move into adolescence.

Table 1.1. Summary of childhood messages

	Tells her . . .	**Tells him . . .**
The family's selection of toys and division of labor	to focus inside the home on the daily care of the house and children	to focus outside the home on accruing financial resources since you are only needed at home sporadically
The church	people like you support those who lead	people like you lead
The education system	your success in "masculine" domains is tied to your effort and is tenuous; achievements of people like you aren't recorded in textbooks	your success in "masculine" domains is tied to your essence and is stable; achievements of people like you are recorded in textbooks
The English language	you are an exception to the norm, not the main player	you are the norm, the main player
Media	people like you are vulnerable and needy	people like you are brave and heroic

In the next chapter we will examine the adolescent experience and the messages girls and boys are given regarding developmental challenges they now face—identity formation and moral decision making. These messages will further channel the decisions they make about future occupations and the work they do for God.

RECOMMENDED READING

Abdallah, Amy Davis. "How Bible Translation Shapes Our View of Women in God's Story." *Mutuality Blog + Magazine*. December 4, 2017. www.cbeinternational.org/resource/article/mutuality-blog-magazine/how-bible-translation-shapes-our-view-women-gods-story.

Devries, Daniel. "Delighting in Fatherhood: Four Ways for Dads to Embrace Nurturing." *Mutuality Blog + Magazine*. March 4, 2017. www.cbeinternational.org/resource/article/mutuality-blog-magazine/delighting-fatherhood-four-ways-dads-embrace-nurturing.

Fine, Cordelia. *Delusions of Gender: How Our Minds, Society, and Neurosexism Create Difference*. New York: W. W. Norton, 2011.

Sathyanesan, Aaron. "A Father's Brain: Four Ways Fatherhood Affects the Brain." *Mutuality Blog + Magazine*. March 4, 2017. www.cbeinternational.org/resource/article/mutuality-blog-magazine/fathers-brain-four-ways-fatherhood-affects-brain.

Yong, Ed. "6-Year-Old Girls Already Have Gendered Beliefs About Intelligence." *The Atlantic*. January 26, 2017. www.theatlantic.com/science/archive/2017/01/six-year-old-girls-already-have-gendered-beliefs-about-intelligence/514340.

2

GENDERED SOCIALIZATION IN ADOLESCENCE

DURING ADOLESCENCE, children transition into adulthood. Physical changes along with the tendency to exaggerate self-perceived flaws create concern in teenagers about how they are perceived by others. Society's sexualization of adolescent girls elicits their concern about the social cost of academic achievement. Identity formation moves to the forefront and their ability to reason through moral dilemmas matures. These changes will help them make a host of choices, including the occupation to which they will devote themselves as adults. Meanwhile, the socialization described in the last chapter continues and shapes the way their identity and moral reasoning unfold. In this chapter, we will explore the adolescent experience and how it helps or hinders the choices these teens make for their life's work.

ACADEMIC ACHIEVEMENT

In elementary school, girls often receive fewer affirmations for their ability in math. They are often told their success in math is tenuous, based more on effort than talent. From the household division of labor to the toys, books, and movies that entertain them, they often learn that their future will involve more time at home and less in the professions requiring math and science skills.

In early adolescence, another reason emerges for these girls to pull away from these subjects. In a study of social self-image among sixth graders, higher math grades were correlated with increases in social self-image for both sexes.[1] However, in the transition from seventh to eighth grade, something changed. Whereas the correlation for boys continued, the girls' self-image improved more when their grades *decreased*.[2] Not by a lot—but when their grades dipped slightly, going from As to Bs, their self-image improved more than that of girls who continued making As.[3] The researchers suggest that socially oriented girls and boys might attempt to improve their social self-image by curtailing mathematical achievement.[4]

These middle-schoolers evidently believe they must choose between achievement and social image. And, evidently, they aren't mistaken. In another study, eighth graders rated pictures of women in STEM careers as more intelligent, more creative, but less attractive than those in non-STEM fields.[5]

Is it any surprise that this concern surfaces at this point for these girls? With adolescence, their bodies are changing, and they are sexualized in ways they haven't been before.[6] Magazines marketed to them are filled with ways to get a boy's interest, clear up their skin, and find that perfect shade of lipstick for this year's

[1]Laura R. Roberts and Anne C. Petersen, "The Relationship Between Academic Achievement and Social Self-Image During Early Adolescence," *Journal of Early Adolescence* 12, no. 2 (1992): 205.

[2]Roberts and Petersen, "Relationship Between Academic Achievement," 205.

[3]Roberts and Petersen, "Relationship Between Academic Achievement," 205.

[4]Roberts and Petersen, "Relationship Between Academic Achievement," 214.

[5]S. Cho et al., "Images of Women in STEM Fields," *Journal of Science Communication* 8, no. 3 (2009): 4.

[6]For information on the sexualization of girls and its effect on identity formation, gender role beliefs, and achievement, see the American Psychological Association, "Report of the APA Task Force on the Sexualization of Girls" (2007), www.apa.org/pi/women/programs/girls/report-full.pdf.

back-to-school fashions. Few convey the importance of math and science to open doors for high-paying, high-status careers. Advertisements on social media and television remind them of their weight, the importance of smiling, and beauty products to create the look they want.

Girls are consistently reminded to be about the business of attracting the opposite sex. They have heard the taunts enough to know boys are shamed for being ousted by a girl, at least in areas in which boys are supposed to shine. If he's insulted when told he runs like a girl, he certainly won't like the girl who beats him in math. Maybe she better hold back. Just a little. Not enough to fail. Just enough to *not* make the A.

But won't this be difficult? To not do her best? To sacrifice her own achievement just to be liked?

Yes.

In fact, adolescence is precisely the point at which the first gender differences in depression appear. While depression is equally prevalent in girls and boys prior to puberty, it is more common in girls beginning with adolescence and continues to be more prevalent in women throughout adulthood.[7] While biology is likely a factor, the evidence is not clear cut.[8] After an extensive crosscultural study, the World Health Organization reported fewer gender differences in depression

[7]For information on depression in adolescence, see R. H. Salk, J. S. Hyde, and L. Y. Abramson, "Gender Differences in Depression in Representative National Samples: Meta-Analyses of Diagnoses and Symptoms," *Psychological Bulletin* 143, no. 8 (2017): 783, and Jean M. Twenge and Susan Nolen-Hoeksema, "Age, Gender, Race, Socioeconomic Status, and Birth Cohort Differences on the Children's Depression Inventory: A Meta-Analysis," *Journal of Abnormal Psychology* 111, no. 4 (2002): 578. For information on depression in adults, see Sucharita Maji, "Society and 'Good Woman': A Critical Review of Gender Difference in Depression," *International Journal of Social Psychiatry*, March 30, 2018; R. H. Salk et al., "Gender Differences," 783; and Anita Riecher-Rossler, "Sex and Gender Differences in Mental Disorders," *The Lancet* 4, January 2017, www.thelancet.com/journals/lanpsy/article/PIIS2215-0366(16)30348-0/fulltext.

[8]Maji, "Society and 'Good Woman'"; and Francesco Acciai and Melissa Hardy, "Depression in Later Life: A Closer Look at the Gender Gap," *Social Science Research* 68 (2017): 163.

in times and places where gender roles are more equal,[9] suggesting that the oppression of women is at least partly responsible.

For these girls, this is only the beginning. As we will examine in the next chapter, their hesitancy to achieve often continues through high school and college and can have consequences for their motivation to enter occupations dominated by men.

IDENTITY FORMATION AND ITS ROLE IN EARLY AND MIDDLE ADULTHOOD

Identity formation. Much of what we know about identity formation comes through the research of psychologist Erik Erikson. His eight-stage theory of psychosocial development encompasses the lifespan, with each stage building on those already accomplished.[10] The stages most relevant for our examination of achievement motivation are (1) identity formation, (2) commitment to intimacy with another person, and (3) generativity, in which the middle-aged adult invests in the well-being of others.[11] An overview of these stages will provide a foundation for us to explore the impact of identity, or lack thereof, on achievement motivation in adulthood.

Although Erikson acknowledged the difficulty in defining identity, he conceptualized it as what William James, father of American psychology, calls character, that is, "the mental or moral attitude in which . . . [one feels] most deeply and intensely active and alive" wherein "a voice inside . . . says: 'This is the real me!'"[12]

While identity formation is a lifelong process, Erikson maintained that it is particularly important during adolescence.[13] To develop a

[9]Soraya Seedat et al., "Cross-national Associations Between Gender and Mental Disorders in the World Health Organization World Mental Health Surveys," *Arch Gen Psychiatry* 66, no. 7 (2009): 793.
[10]Erik H. Erikson, *The Life Cycle Completed: A Review* (New York: W. W. Norton, 1982), 56-57, 66.
[11]Erikson, *Life Cycle Completed*, 56-57, 67.
[12]Erik H. Erikson, *Identity: Youth and Crisis* (New York: W. W. Norton, 1968), 15, 19-20.
[13]Erikson, *Identity*, 23-24.

sense of self, teenagers often challenge the ways of previous generations,[14] such as their religious views, political ideologies, clothing styles, and music preferences. Ideally, this exploration helps these young people decide who they are apart from who others say they are or wish them to be. This identity will become the basis for their choice of friends and life partner, the religious and political ideologies they embrace, the code of conduct by which they make decisions, the leisure activities they find worthwhile, and where to invest themselves occupationally.

Yet none of these decisions are made free of childhood socialization. In fact, we might expect for boys and girls to enter adolescence with different behavior patterns stemming from a history of sex-typed messages that have already set limits on their choices, whether they will form an identity, and the shape that identity will take.

The girl, for instance, enters adolescence with over a decade of messages that tend to steer her toward home and childcare and away from achievement elsewhere. *Babies, the kitchen, and vacuum cleaners are your domain. People like you rarely achieve in ways the world notices, and when they do, they pay a price. Better tone down your success if you want him to like you. Wear the right makeup. Have the perfect body. Oh, and don't forget to smile!* As one woman told me, "A career . . . was spoken of as something to be careful of, because it was understood that being a mom . . . was the best choice." The degree to which the girl buys into those messages will affect whether she develops an identity easily or at all.

The boy, however, enters adolescence with a very different set of messages. *You are one of the world's achievers; your accomplishments will be recorded in books. You can do this because your work at home is peripheral, anyway. Someone else will care for your children and*

---

[14]Erikson, *Identity*, 27-28.

make sure you have meals and clean clothes. And go ahead—be smart! It will make you more successful. The degree to which he has bought into these will affect his development of an identity. What seems, on the surface, to be freedom among limitless options too often is one set of options for those who will achieve and another set for those who will help someone else achieve.

Early adulthood. An identity is a reservoir from which we draw to form and maintain close, meaningful relationships. Those who have an identity are in the position to build an intimate relationship with another, one that involves "the capacity to commit . . . to concrete affiliations which may call for significant sacrifices and compromises."[15] For those who do not, intimacy will be elusive. Critics of Erikson's theory, however, maintain that some, especially women, do achieve intimacy without an identity.[16]

While theorists debate this, my experience as a psychologist and mentor of young adults suggests that successful intimacy is most likely when each individual has a clear sense of who they are and what they want in life. But when one of those persons, usually the woman, has been taught to seek her identity in a spouse and children, then accepting her spouse's identity as her own seems the most expedient way to build intimacy. His values become her values. His wishes dominate and dictate the direction their lives will take.

This wife is then applauded as agreeable, submissive, and respectful of her husband's leadership. But I suspect that this agreeable, respectful submission too often stems from the lack of a complete identity. To follow what her culture—both religious and secular—has prescribed as the woman's role, she has neglected to develop herself fully. Without a sense of who she is apart from her husband,

---

[15]Erikson, *Life Cycle Completed*, 70, 72.

[16]David R. Matteson, "Differences Within and Between Genders: A Challenge to the Theory," in *Ego Identity: A Handbook for Psychosocial Research*, ed. J. E. Marcia et al. (New York: Springer-Verlag, 1993), 83-85.

she won't ascribe as much importance to her own desires, much less a call that arises from an identity uniquely her own. She won't consider that the discontent she feels could be God nudging her toward wholeness. That God might use her talents to guide the choices of her family will not occur to her, much less weigh in as a factor in family decisions.

When my husband and I were newlyweds, we lived in the city where he attended seminary. Although I looked forward to graduate training, I hadn't yet determined where to go nor which program to pursue. It made sense, I told myself, for him to go first. He would study while I worked to support us and took time to choose a school and program for myself.

I had several friends in the same situation and spoke with them occasionally about my plans to attend school when my husband finished. I assumed they would do the same. After all, we had spent our college days studying and planning for the careers we would pursue. Why not follow through? More than one of them told me we couldn't make plans yet since we didn't know where God would call our husbands. We would have to wait and see.

My students will find it hard to imagine that, at first, I believed those words: I would have to wait and see. But it bothered me. I couldn't let it go. I had studied hard and prayed for years about my professional plans. I read everything about psychology I could get my hands on. I pored over graduate school catalogs while I dreamed of the classes I would take, the skills I would hone, the clients I would treat. Was I supposed to wait and hope my husband would find a church close to a school with a graduate program in psychology?

While I believed God could work through that situation, that wasn't at all the way we had approached my husband's education. For his, we trusted that what he believed was a call was just that. We took that call seriously and moved to the place where he could get the education to live it out. We didn't wait and hope I would find a job in a town with a graduate program for ministers. We didn't wait to see what God had in store for me first. We didn't even read a book that encouraged him to uncover buried talents.

We did none of that. We simply trusted and took action.

I am happy to report that since I couldn't let it go, I didn't. One night I broached the topic with my husband. I told him that we had taken three years to invest in his life's work and that before he took a church that would require a move, I wanted to get my master's degree. I admit I felt a bit heretical. If he had asked me to defend my position, I'm not sure I could have. I just knew it felt right and needed to be said.

Imagine my surprise when he said, "Sure."

Of course I should pursue my calling. And what would he do while I studied? We didn't know. Just do what I had done for him, we supposed. Work in a job, either in his area or not depending on what he could find, and put off better options until we could both relocate.

I was pleasantly surprised and, I admit, relieved. His commitment to my call equaled my commitment to his.

If he had refused, I believe I would have stood my ground. My identity was solid. But even so, stating what I wanted and asking for his support was difficult. Why? Because my culture—secular and religious—had taught me that to a great extent my identity was to be found in him—that I was to focus less on pursuing my own achievement and more on supporting his. Without an identity, it would have been difficult to even have this conversation much less counter his arguments if he had objected. It would have been much easier to get in line with his plans and forget my own.

Forming an identity that keeps you on course through adulthood is an important task and difficult for many. However, it is more difficult for the woman who is primed to take on the dreams of her husband. Without an identity, she will be at risk for ignoring her own dreams and failing to achieve her full potential.

Middle adulthood. Those who develop an identity and achieve intimacy are then ready for the middle adulthood stage, which centers on contributing to others' well-being (see table 2.1). Ways to accomplish this generativity[17] are varied, and often come through raising children, leisure activities, and occupational pursuits, including ministry. Passing on one's values and heritage to children, mentoring young professionals at work, leading a youth group at church, coaching youth sports, building houses for the needy, volunteering time to a political campaign—the opportunities are limitless.

Table 2.1. Erik Erikson's psychosocial stages of identity, intimacy, and generativity

Adolescence	Identity formation	Developing a sense of self
Early adulthood	Intimacy	Achieving intimacy with another
Middle adulthood	Generativity	Productivity, caring for others
Source: Erikson, *Life Cycle Completed*, 32-33, 67, 73.		

One might expect that individuals who have formed an identity—know themselves, what they stand for and can offer—are in the best position to contribute in ways consistent with their chosen values, to bring the best of themselves into alignment with the needs of the world. Those who have taken on another's identity might find it difficult to plug into the world's needs in a way that feels true to themselves.

The woman who has gifts and a call that would take her into more global service might find work at home unsatisfying, her days incomplete, even when busily caring for a husband and children she loves dearly. She will be reprimanded for downplaying the

[17]Erikson, *Life Cycle Completed*, 67.

importance of work she does for her family. Do it gladly, her church friends will tell her, "as working for the Lord" (Colossians 3:23). Others will recommend she get a part-time job to get out of the house and fill her days. I suggest, however, that she needs to ponder whether she is called to achieve something bigger than she has been socialized to expect or has allowed herself to consider.

An identity is broader than any occupation. Who we *are* transcends what we *do*. However, the choices we make regarding how to spend forty hours a week for roughly four decades will have a tremendous impact on how that identity unfolds over the course of a lifetime. And it will undoubtedly influence the scope of our contributions during middle adulthood if we limit ourselves to the expectations imposed by our culture. For the woman who is not restrained in such a way, free to proceed according to ability and talent, her service will be as far-reaching as God's call takes her.

MORAL REASONING

A sense of right and wrong begins to develop before children enter school, certainly much earlier than adolescence. However, during the teen years, moral reasoning takes on special significance as the adolescent is creating an identity and taking the first steps toward occupational goals. In this section, we will explore the theories of Lawrence Kohlberg and Carol Gilligan and examine their implications for how boys and girls use moral reasoning to make achievement-related decisions. We will also consider the impact of those decisions for their adult lives.

Lawrence Kohlberg's research explored the reasoning his participants used when presented with moral dilemmas.[18] One classic dilemma involved a man named Heinz who stole a drug he could not

[18]Lawrence Kohlberg, *Essays on Moral Development*, vol. 1, *The Philosophy of Moral Development: Moral Stages and the Idea of Justice* (San Francisco, Harper and Row, 1981), 16.

afford to save the life of his sick wife.[19] At the first level of reasoning, referred to as the *preconventional* level, self-interest determined whether a behavior was judged to be moral or immoral.[20] For instance, the participants showed concern for the consequences likely to ensue for Heinz if he stole, or did not steal, the drug.

The second level, referred to as *conventional* morality, is characterized by a desire to meet others' standards.[21] Two stages comprise this level. In one, the person focuses on concern for others, being good, and following the rules within individual relationships.[22] Whether he should steal to save a life would depend on what a good person would do and how other people would judge him. In the next, slightly more advanced, stage the rules set forth by systems or institutions carry more weight.[23] Someone at this stage might base a decision on what the government or church says is right. Fulfilling one's duty and maintaining the social order are important at this level.[24] Kohlberg found this stage of the second level to be the most common among adults.[25]

Those who continue to the third and final level, however, gauge morality by mutually agreed on social contracts that advance the greatest good for the greatest number of people.[26] This level assumes the value of some principles (such as the inherent value of life and liberty), even when they contradict the law.[27]

While Kohlberg's theory is well respected, the fact that his participants were all boys and men brought into question whether his

---

[19]Georg Lind, "Measuring Moral Judgment: A Review of *The Measurement of Moral Judgment* by Anne Colby and Lawrence Kohlberg," *Human Development* 32 (1989): 391.
[20]Kohlberg, *Essays on Moral Development*, 409.
[21]Kohlberg, *Essays on Moral Development*, 410.
[22]Kohlberg, *Essays on Moral Development*, 410.
[23]Kohlberg, *Essays on Moral Development*, 410-11.
[24]Kohlberg, *Essays on Moral Development*, 410.
[25]Kohlberg, *Essays on Moral Development*, 151.
[26]Kohlberg, *Essays on Moral Development*, 411-12.
[27]Kohlberg, *Essays on Moral Development*, 411-12.

findings adequately reflected the reasoning of girls and women. Carol Gilligan didn't think so. In attending to the female experience, her research brought to light the centrality of care and relationships in moral reasoning.[28] She proposed that females, like males, begin with self-interest but then move toward self-sacrifice as a gauge for morality.[29] The right choice at this level would be one of self-denial in order to serve others. In the third and final level, rather than seeking self-interest or self-sacrifice, women consider their own needs alongside the needs of others when searching for a solution.[30]

Yet Gilligan herself stated that while differences exist in the way individuals approach moral decision making, sex isn't necessarily the distinguishing factor.[31] Instead, she suggested, social status and power weigh in, along with sex, in moral reasoning.[32] Her caution seems warranted given research that found men only slightly more likely to use the orientation described by Kohlberg and women only slightly more likely to use the orientation described by Gilligan.[33]

While differences exist between the two theories, I suggest an important similarity relevant to the achievement striving of women. With each orientation, responsibility for determining right and wrong shifts from self-interest to a focus on external sources (others' needs, opinions, or institutionalized rules) and finally to a more objective consideration of all concerned. The greatest good for the greatest number, of which Kohlberg speaks, echoes the balancing of one's own needs with those of others, emphasized by Gilligan. With each orientation, the pinnacle of morality requires that the good of

[28]Carol Gilligan, *In a Different Voice: Psychological Theory and Women's Development* (Cambridge, MA: Harvard University Press, 1993), 30-31.
[29]Gilligan, *In a Different Voice*, 74.
[30]Gilligan, *In a Different Voice*, 149.
[31]Gilligan, *In a Different Voice*, 2.
[32]Gilligan, *In a Different Voice*, 2.
[33]Sara Jaffee and Janet Shibley Hyde, "Gender Differences in Moral Orientation: A Meta-Analysis," *Psychological Bulletin* 126, no. 5 (2000): 703.

all outweighs both self-interest and an unmitigated obligation to others.

How does this relate to achievement? First, societal forces (i.e., status, power, and expectations) rather than biological sex per se seem to be the basis for differences in the way men and women reason and subsequently make moral decisions. Second, according to Kohlberg's research, most remain at the conventional level where others' opinions carry more weight than self-interest or abstract principles. Therefore, we can expect that when making occupational decisions and navigating how these decisions will affect the marriage relationship, women and men will be influenced more by what others say than by the principles they endorse. Even for the couple who values equality, who espouses the supremacy of God's will over earthly governments, who takes pride in listening to God's voice over those of the world—even *those* couples will find it difficult to counter the voices of family and friends, pastors, and political leaders who urge them to maintain the social order.

Let's consider, then, the teenage boy who is making choices about his future. He will move through adolescence and into adulthood with a choir of voices—caregivers, parents, teachers, friends, and church leaders—urging him to achieve. The institutionalized voices of this choir chime in with the same message: *leaders are people like you*. When deciding whether to pursue a position of leadership, he doesn't have to be convinced that it's an appropriate, moral option. The people and institutions that have molded him have told him all along that he is achievement material and will likely have a spouse to support him in this endeavor. Since she will be the primary caregiver for their children and responsible for household upkeep, he won't be shirking any responsibilities on the home front. But even if it comes to that, his primary obligation will be to God, so his wife will be okay with that. At least she *should* be if she's a good wife.

The choir will sing a different tune, however, for the teenage girl, one that urges her to make decisions based on what others need from her. She is encouraged to achieve but only in ways that will not interfere with supporting her husband's dreams and being the primary caregiver of their children. If she feels called to leadership herself, she will be encouraged to consider what it will mean for her husband and children. What will they have to sacrifice if she pursues her dreams?

Few women will consider it appropriate to require as much sacrifice from a husband as they are willing to make for him. Few men will adhere to an underlying principle if it means they must go against the dictates of the church, an institution which has historically worked to keep women out of leadership.

As a student at a Baptist college in the 1980s, I knew a lot of men preparing for the pastorate. Like many of my friends who were dating them, I knew I would one day become a pastor's wife. I knew this would require a lot of my time and involvement in the churches my husband pastored and that my role would be critical to his success in ministry. I would be under constant scrutiny. Could I choose my words and actions wisely? Was I prepared to support him through my devoted (and unpaid) service to his congregations? Would I graciously uproot if God called him to serve in another community? Would this hinder my career? *Would I support rather than hinder my future spouse's ministry?* My friends and I asked these questions as we considered life with our future husbands.

Yet, to my knowledge, "Will you support, rather than hinder, your future *wife's* calling?" was seldom asked of these men. We assumed God called men to ministry and called women to support their husbands' call. Few of us, myself included, questioned that assumption. We had heard it taught in every church we had attended and confirmed by our culture at large. The greatest good for the greatest number didn't include pastors' wives, did it? How would two calls even work? Balancing both would probably limit his call, wouldn't it? We were following mandates of both the church and society that to make wise, moral choices meant we follow institutional rules and that self-sacrifice (at least for us women) should be the gauge.

Of course, there are exceptions. Some individuals look beyond the self-interest of level one and the self-sacrifice of level two, meaning they will be less likely to cling to self-interest or pay undue attention to what their friends, families, or institutions tout as the moral choice. Rather, they look for an underlying principle to direct their behavior, or as Gilligan found, seek balance between the needs of each person involved (see table 2.2). I know couples who have actively worked toward this goal. One friend told me that she and her boyfriend discussed her plans for ministry alongside his, including their mutual willingness to sacrifice for the other's goals. Another told me that even though they faced a fair amount of backlash from friends and family who did not understand their going against tradition, they stayed the course to do what they believed was right.

Am I saying that couples who live out a more traditional style of marriage are morally deficient? Of course not. I know several women who have served in a supporting role for their husbands after examining all options and with due consideration for the needs of each person involved. Some women find their call and goals are not minimized in this style of marriage. The goal isn't for all couples to forsake the traditional system; it undoubtedly works well for many.

However, for so many capable women to not make it to higher levels of leadership within the church, educational institutions, or other organizations suggests that the scales are tipped in a way that creates undue hindrance to these women. All institutions, the church included, will be better served if all people, women and men, bring the best of who we are to God's service.

Table 2.2. Decision making at each level of moral reasoning

Lawrence Kohlberg's stages of moral development[a]	Decisions about calling	Carol Gilligan's stages of moral development[b]
Level 1 Behavior is moral if it serves self-interest.		**Level 1** Behavior is moral if it serves self-interest.
Level 2 Behavior is moral if it conforms to others' standards: first, to the rules within individual relationships, and later, to the standards set by systems and institutions, fulfilling one's duty, and maintaining the social order.	Couples at this level will prioritize the husband's call over the wife's as they conform to the expectations of friends and family and to standards of the church and other institutions; the wife deems her self-sacrifice and service to others as the measure of morality.	**Level 2** The moral choice is one of self-sacrifice, self-denial, service to others.
Level 3 Behavior is moral if it upholds social contracts that serve the greatest good for the greatest number, even when that contradicts the law.	Couples at this level will move beyond self-interest, self-denial, and conformity to others' expectations as they make decisions with due consideration for both the husband's and the wife's call (i.e., the greatest good for the greatest number).	**Level 3** The moral choice is one that considers one's own needs and wishes alongside the needs and wishes of others.

[a]Kohlberg, *Essays on Moral Development*, 409-12.
[b]Gilligan, *In a Different Voice*, 74, 149.

In summary, adolescence ushers in a pressing need to form an identity and an increased ability to reason through moral choices. Specifically, girls are often encouraged to make choices based on self-sacrifice and to focus more on a future spouse's achievements than on their own. Boys, however, are often told that achievement is a worthwhile goal for themselves and are led to expect spousal support. These gender differences in socialization present obstacles to women fully embracing a call that involves leadership (see table 2.3). In the next chapter, we will explore how this socialization continues into adulthood to further impact their occupational plans.

Table 2.3. Summary of adolescent messages

	Tells her . . .	**Tells him . . .**
Academic success	being smart will make you less likeable	being smart will make you more likeable
Identity formation	your identity is to be a support system for someone else's accomplishments	your identity is tied to your accomplishments
Moral development	the moral choice is to follow the regulations of others which say to self-sacrifice	the moral choice is to follow the regulations of others which say to accomplish

RECOMMENDED READING

Calhoun, Adele Ahlberg, and Tracey D. Bianchi. *True You: Overcoming Self-Doubt and Using Your Voice*. Downers Grove, IL: InterVarsity Press, 2014.

De Souza, Becca. "My Body Kept Score: What Purity Culture Didn't Know About Trauma." CBE Blog/Magazine. January 27, 2021. www.cbeinternational.org/resource/article/mutuality-blog-magazine/my-body-kept-score-what-purity-culture-didnt-know-about.

Johns, Cheryl Bridges. *Seven Transforming Gifts of Menopause: An Unexpected Spiritual Journey*. Grand Rapids, MI: Brazos, 2020.

LaCelle-Peterson, Kristina. *Liberating Tradition: Women's Identity and Vocation in Christian Perspective*. Grand Rapids, MI: Baker Academic, 2008.

Mathews, Alice P. *Preaching That Speaks to Women*. Grand Rapids, MI: Baker Academic, 2003.

Van Leeuwen, Mary Stewart. *My Brother's Keeper: What the Social Sciences Do (and Don't) Tell Us About Masculinity*. Downer's Grove, IL: IVP Academic, 2002.

3 GENDERED SOCIALIZATION IN ADULTHOOD

By the time adolescents reach adulthood, they have had almost two decades of messages regarding their abilities, the opportunities they can expect as men and women, and the best way to choose among them. In this chapter, we will consider another channel of gendered socialization for these individuals who are now adults—the expectations they encounter as they move into positions of leadership. We will also examine two gender differences that serve to fortify their occupational choices—their communication patterns and differences in the way they gauge success.

GENDERED EXPECTATIONS FOR LEADERSHIP

While becoming an effective leader can be a challenge for anyone, women who embark on this journey face an obstacle that men do not: namely, the competing expectations of the female gender role and those of being an effective leader. Role congruity theory suggests that for a woman to be perceived as a good leader, she must embody agentic qualities (e.g., decisiveness, assertiveness, directness) that are inconsistent with the female gender role.[1] If she

[1]See the initial research on role congruity theory in Alice H. Eagly and Seven J. Karau, "Role Congruity Theory of Prejudice Toward Female Leaders," *Psychological Review* 109, no. 3

exhibits communal qualities associated with the female role (e.g., nurturance, cooperation, sensitivity), she is not perceived to be leadership material.[2] Yet, her display of agentic qualities associated with leadership is met with disapproval and lack of cooperation, which can *also* impede her attempts to lead.[3]

Some research shows that men exhibit more bias related to gender-role congruity than do women in jobs that are traditionally held by men.[4] This bias led Koch et al. to conclude that "men may be sensitive to changes in the traditional gender hierarchy and may disapprove of women working in male-dominated, high-status occupations."[5] With men often being the gatekeepers for such positions, their bias will be especially problematic for these women.

So, what is the answer? Eagly and Karau suggest that exhibiting communal along with agentic behaviors might mediate the negative reactions women receive to their agency "as long as these behaviors do not violate the relevant leadership role."[6] Likewise, Schock et al. found that those most often identified as having leadership potential were those for whom "the relative numbers of agentic and communal characteristics specified by peers were balanced."[7]

(2002): 573. In addition, see Tamer Koburtay, Jawad Syed, and Radi Haloub, "Congruity Between the Female Gender Role and the Leader Role: A Literature Review," *European Business Review* 31, no. 6 (2019): 841.

[2]Eagly and Karau, "Role Congruity Theory," 590.

[3]Eagly and Karau, "Role Congruity Theory," 590. For information on intersectionality as it relates to role congruity theory, see Robert W. Livingston, Ashleigh Shelby Rosette, and Ella F. Washington, "Can an Agentic Black Woman Get Ahead? The Impact of Race and Interpersonal Dominance on Perceptions of Female Leaders," *Psychological Science* 23, no. 4 (2012): 354-58. In essence, Black women and White men are not subjected to the same role congruity bias that is experienced by White women and Black men.

[4]Amanda J. Koch, Susan D. D'Mello, and Paul R. Sackett, "A Meta-Analysis of Gender Stereotypes and Bias in Experimental Simulations of Employment Decision Making," *Journal of Applied Psychology 100*, no. 1 (2015): 139. Warren Whisenant, Debbiesiu L. Lee, and Windy Dees, "Role Congruity Theory: Perceptions of Fairness and Sexism in Sport Management," *Public Organization Review* 15 (2015): 483.

[5]Koch, D'Mello, and Sackett, "Meta-Analysis of Gender Stereotypes," 139.

[6]Eagly and Karau, "Role Congruity Theory," 590.

[7]Anne-Kathrin Schock et al., "Tempering Agency with Communion Increases Women's Leadership Emergence in All-Women Groups: Evidence for Role Congruity Theory in a

Yet expanding one's behavioral repertoire isn't without problems. Eagly and Karau caution that while doing so might help women garner acceptance, "it may compromise their advancement to higher level positions because their behavior may appear less powerful and confident than that of their male counterparts."[8] Similarly, Khattab and Leroy report that women (but not men) who lead using both agentic and communal behaviors are seen as less authentic, which is unfortunate since perceptions of authenticity mediate the perception of being an effective leader.[9]

Regardless of the accommodations women are advised to employ, the result is that women are held to a different set of expectations than are their male counterparts. The complexity of such a task is evident in the conclusion drawn by Schock and colleagues: "Women are called upon to enhance their self-awareness to adopt an advantageous blend of agentic and communal types of behavior and use it strategically. Given both the importance of agentic behaviors for claiming a leadership position in the first place and the importance of communal behaviors for avoiding backlash effects, it is appropriate to address both aspects."[10]

Keep in mind that this double bind exists in the absence of actual gender differences in leadership ability.[11] As Cynthia Kubu puts it, "The data overwhelmingly indicate that good and effective leaders tend to be good and effective leaders regardless of gender."[12] Yet, perceptions of her ability continue to pose obstacles for women who journey toward fulfilling their call.

Field Setting," *The Leadership Quarterly* 30 (2019): 194. While this research was conducted using only women, findings were consistent with the research of Eagly and Karau.

[8]Eagly and Karau, "Role Congruity Theory," 590.

[9]Jasmien Khattab and Hannes Leroy, "An Authenticity Approach to Role Congruity Theory," *Proceedings of the Academy of Management*, November 30, 2017.

[10]Schock et al., "Tempering Agency with Communion," 196.

[11]Cynthia S. Kubu, "Who Does She Think She Is? Women, Leadership and the 'B'(ias) Word," *The Clinical Neuropsychologist* 32, no. 2 (2018): 235.

[12]Kubu, "Who Does She Think She Is?," 239.

GENDERED COMMUNICATION

Woman: I'm thinking maybe we could have Mexican tonight. What do you think?

Man: I'm tired of Mexican. I want Chinese.

Woman: We could do that, I guess.

What will it be tonight—egg rolls or burritos? I'm betting on egg rolls. Why? Because he clearly stated what he wanted. She hedged, communicating that she wasn't sure and wanted him to weigh in. (She will later complain that she never gets to pick the restaurant. He will be confused because she rarely seems to care where they eat.)

While most communication patterns of men and women are quite similar,[13] differences also exist. Men's speech tends to be more direct, with the use of directives ("Hand me the book") and succinct statements; women's speech less so, as characterized by greater use of uncertainty verbs ("It looks like . . .") and hedges ("I'd sort of like to . . .").[14]

While this pattern creates an imbalance and eventual conflict around mealtime, it will also repeat itself in more serious discussions. For instance, when they talk over whether they should relocate for his job or for hers, it will surface again.

Man: "This position will mean more hours, but the pay is better. I want to take it."

Woman: "It might be good for my career. How do you feel about me working more hours?"

My guess is: they'll move for his work, not hers. Why? Because his direct statement communicates a confidence that hers lacks.

Different communication styles create risks too numerous for this chapter. But to focus on the topic at hand, this difference means his

---

[13]Anthony Mulac, "The Gender-Linked Language Effect: Do Language Differences Really Make a Difference?," in *Sex Differences and Similarities in Communication*, 2nd ed., ed. Daniel J. Canary and Kathryn Dindia (New York: Routledge, 2006), 222.

[14]Mulac, "Gender-Linked Language," 225, 227.

call will be voiced more clearly and, therefore, understood by *his* spouse more often than her call will be voiced and understood by *her* spouse. The result? His call will be better defined, taken more seriously, supported more consistently, and lived out more fully than hers.

However, consequences go beyond their communication with each other. One study found that observers of language differences, without knowing the gender of those they were rating, judged the men to be stronger and the women to be nicer.[15] Consider, then, the church committee or the board of a company interviewing a man and a woman for a position of leadership. The male candidate will communicate strength and thus appear more confident. And, although they will give her credit for being nice, they will judge her as being less sure of herself. So, who do you predict will get the job?

This happened with an acquaintance of mine who interviewed for a leadership position within a nonprofit organization. The committee told her later that they assumed she didn't want the job, so they went with the other candidate, a man, who they believed *did* want the job. She had, in fact, refrained from stating that she was called to be their leader. But what she intended as respect for their discernment regarding whom to hire, they interpreted as her lacking confidence in her call! Was he more confident than she? I don't know. But committee members thought so and that, ultimately, was critical to their decision.

Although patterns of communication differ, where those differences originate is less clear. However, for us to acquire these patterns through gendered enculturation makes intuitive sense. Consistent messages that encourage boys to own their success and discourage the same in girls might foster different levels of confidence (or at least the *appearance* of such) between the sexes.

---

[15]Mulac, "Gender-Linked Language," 237.

Of course, variations exist among men and among women. Plenty of women, myself included, are direct. Plenty of men are not. Research indicates patterns, not perfect correlations. However, to let patterns go unaddressed because there are exceptions would be negligent, especially when those patterns have implications for the life work of half the population.

THE GAUGE OF SUCCESS

College students were asked a series of questions to determine the level of importance they attached to each of the following in terms of feeling good about themselves: (1) self-perceived competence (personal knowledge of doing a good job), (2) reflected appraisals (affirmation from others), or (3) social comparisons (doing better than someone else).[16] The study indicated that self-perceived competence is equally important to men and women, with reflected appraisals weighing in as the most important factor for both sexes.[17] However, it showed that women place slightly more importance than men do on reflected appraisals; men, more than women, rely on social comparison.[18]

In addition to relying less on social comparison, another study found that women might actually *avoid* being singled out for their achievements. When asked to predict their grade point average (GPA) in a public setting with those whose GPA was lower, women voiced lower grades than did the men, even though the GPAs of these men and women were similar.[19] These women seemed to be concerned about the other person's feelings.[20] In another study, women believed that other women didn't like them as much when

---

[16]Michael L. Schwalbe and Clifford L. Staples, "Gender Differences in Sources of Self-Esteem," *Social Psychology Quarterly* 54, no. 2 (1991): 162.

[17]Schwalbe and Staples, "Gender Differences in Sources of Self-Esteem," 162-63.

[18]Schwalbe and Staples, "Gender Differences in Sources of Self-Esteem," 163.

[19]Laurie Heatherington et al., "Two Investigations of 'Female Modesty' in Achievement Situations," *Sex Roles* 29, no. 11/12 (1993): 739.

[20]Heatherington et al., "Two Investigations of 'Female Modesty,'" 739-40.

they bragged about a test grade.[21] In fact, they believed that if the woman had not done well herself, she might be upset and feel worse about herself.[22]

Several years ago, before I had read any of this research, I had an experience that illustrated this perfectly. I love board games and had gotten really good at one in particular. One evening a friend came over and wanted to learn the game. I told her the rules, gave her a few tips on strategy, and we played. About halfway through, I realized I was holding back from playing as well as I could have. I didn't mind playing better than she; I had played for a while, so that was to be expected. But I also didn't want to make her feel bad by showing her up. So, I held back—not enough to lose, but enough to level the playing field. When I shared this with a male colleague the next day, he was surprised I had downplayed my skill to spare her feelings. For one person to play better than another is just life, he said, and no reason to hold back.

Interestingly, my colleague's response illustrated another finding of the same study: men did not believe their bragging would reduce their likability.[23] In fact, some thought it would make women like them *more.*[24] These men believed that being open about their success wouldn't harm anyone and might even benefit their relationship with women.

But it doesn't end there. In another study, men were presented with "good" and "bad" items and asked to respond quickly to each one by pressing one of two computer keys depending on whether or not they associated those items with themselves.[25] Their immediate

[21]Kimberly A. Daubman and Harold Sigall, "Gender Differences in Perceptions of How Others Are Affected by Self-Disclosure of Achievement," *Sex Roles* 37, no. 1/2 (1997): 73.

[22]Daubman and Sigall, "Gender Differences in Perceptions," 73.

[23]Daubman and Sigall, "Gender Differences in Perceptions," 84.

[24]Daubman and Sigall, "Gender Differences in Perceptions," 84.

[25]Kate A. Ratliff and Shigehiro Oishi, "Gender Differences in Implicit Self-Esteem Following a Romantic Partner's Success or Failure," *Journal of Personality and Social Psychology* 105, no. 4 (2013): 690-91, https://doi.org/10.1037/a0033769.

reactions in this implicit measure of self-esteem would hopefully reveal feelings about themselves of which they might not even be aware. Before they began, however, these men were asked to think and write about a time when their opposite-sex partner had either succeeded or failed at something.[26]

Results revealed that men's self-esteem was higher when they thought about their partners' failure than when they thought about their success.[27] Thinking about a partner's success might prompt a man to feel bad about himself in comparison, causing his self-esteem to take a hit.[28] If so, being better than someone else is one factor (albeit an unconscious one) that drives male confidence. Interestingly, the same study found that women's self-esteem was unrelated to thoughts about their male partners' successes or failures.[29]

Therefore, if the situation arises—and it will, when she excels at sports in elementary school, makes the top grade in high school, or lands a job that pays more than his—she'll be reminded of the delicate male ego. The reminder will come from her mother or sister or best friend, and often with an eye roll, that his masculinity is at stake and that she better protect it. And she probably will. How do we know? Because, as research indicates, in public settings with someone who has not done as well, she's likely to downplay her own success out of concern for the other person's feelings.

On the surface, this gender difference appears to create a win-win situation for the man and woman in a relationship. He won't see his own success as detrimental to her. And she won't clamor to highlight her own success since that would be bragging and counterproductive to their relationship—which, remember, is central to her moral code and sense of identity.

---

[26]Ratliff and Oishi, "Gender Differences in Implicit Self-Esteem," 692.
[27]Ratliff and Oishi, "Gender Differences in Implicit Self-Esteem," 698.
[28]Ratliff and Oishi, "Gender Differences in Implicit Self-Esteem," 698.
[29]Ratliff and Oishi, "Gender Differences in Implicit Self-Esteem," 698.

But won't this put her at a disadvantage? To make *his* self-esteem *her* problem? Won't that unfairly discourage her from doing as well as she can in the future? Won't this limit the use of her talent, education, and call?

You bet. But keep in mind that reflected appraisals are important for women's self-esteem. And she will receive more positive feedback for adhering to gender-role norms than she will for flouting them.

But does any of this affect occupational achievement? Research on the fear of success in women suggests that it does. The fear of success is the avoidance of situations in which high achievement is possible and likely to evoke negative consequences. In a classic study, college men and women were given a one-sentence prompt and asked to complete the story. Women were given: "After first term finals, Anne finds herself at the top of her medical school class." Men were given the same, except with the name *John* substituted for *Anne*.[30]

Over 90 percent of college men in this sample responded with positive stories, such as John would one day provide well for a wife, have a bright future, or continue to work hard.[31] However, 65 percent of women responded with stories of negative consequences, distress, or confusion.[32] For instance, Anne's success was associated with her loss of femininity, social rejection, or quitting.[33] Like the dilemma of middle-school girls and their math grades, these women predicted a high price for success in areas traditionally dominated by men. By the way, these fears are not without basis as women who achieve in male-dominated careers are liked less and belittled more than equally successful men.[34]

---

[30]Matina S. Horner, "Toward an Understanding of Achievement-Related Conflicts in Women," *Journal of Social Issues* 28, no. 2 (1972): 161.

[31]Ratliff and Oishi, "Gender Differences in Implicit Self-Esteem," 162.

[32]Ratliff and Oishi, "Gender Differences in Implicit Self-Esteem," 162.

[33]Horner, "Toward an Understanding," 162-163

[34]Madeline E. Heilman et al., "Penalties for Success: Reactions to Women Who Succeed at Male Gender-Typed Tasks," *Journal of Applied Psychology* 89, no. 3 (2004): 416.

Let's recap. Others' affirmations are particularly important to women. In a world that sees their primary goal as marriage and motherhood, women are not as likely to receive affirmation for outside-the-home pursuits. This encourages them to focus on home and family rather than an occupation, even one within ministry. While men believe their own success will impress others and confer advantages on a future wife and children, women believe their own success will hurt others and compete with the goal of family. Their fears are not unfounded given that men's self-esteem takes a hit when female partners succeed and women who succeed in male-dominated fields are belittled and seen as unattractive. For men, success is a win-win; for women, it hardly seems in their own best interests (see table 3.1).

Table 3.1. Gender differences in role expectations, communication, and gauging success

Women	Men
Women are expected to meet competing role expectations: those for being female and those for being a leader	Men are expected to meet role expectations that are congruent: those for being male and those for being a leader
Resulting in more criticism for her leadership endeavors, less for his	
Women communicate more with hedging and uncertainty verbs	Men communicate more with succinct directives
Resulting in his call being voiced more clearly and taken more seriously than hers	
Women feel better about themselves when affirmed by others and see their own success as harmful to others and a threat to their future family	Men feel better about themselves when performing better than others and see their own success as impressive to others and advantageous to their future family
Resulting in each of them focusing more on his achievements than on hers	

I regularly hear that while society treats men and women differently, these differences put no one at a disadvantage. We are equal, I'm told, just different. This *separate but equal* argument deemed invalid as a basis for racial segregation is just as invalid for the differential treatment of the sexes. When men believe their success is good for everyone, and women believe their own will exact a price from everyone, when men feel diminished by their wives' success and women downplay their own to have a family, it's difficult to see this as anything less than a disadvantage to women.

The egalitarian interpretation of the fall of humanity provides a spiritual context for the research described in these pages. Frances Hiebert asserts that God's intent for men and women to rule together is evident in God giving both Adam and Eve responsibility to subdue creation (Genesis 1:28).[35] It isn't until the fall that God tells the woman, "Your desire will be for your husband, and he will rule over you" (Genesis 3:16). Rather than an injunction for the sexes to embrace male dominance, here God foreshadows the brokenness that will now characterize the male-female relationship because of sin.[36] Husbands will try to dominate their wives; wives will sacrifice themselves for the sake of relationship, thus "she contributes to the idolatry of the male."[37] Rather than God's intent, the imbalance in the husband-wife relationship is the natural consequence of sin.[38]

In a system in which the husband dominates and the wife dismisses her own calling by allowing his domination, we have quite a different picture of marriage than depicted in the creation account. We no longer have Adam's joy with the one who is "bone of my bones and flesh of my flesh" (Genesis 2:23). Nor do we have two individual identities uniting in the intimacy Erikson described. Instead, we have a broken system in need of redemption.

In light of this interpretation, men feeling good about themselves when they are better than women, and women not using God-given abilities to their fullest in order to please men makes perfect sense.

Along with Hiebert, I propose that all of us—men and women, husbands and wives—work toward redeeming the brokenness that now exists between the sexes.[39] One way to begin is by eradicating

---

[35]Frances Hiebert, "Beginning at the Beginning," *Priscilla Papers* 3, no. 3 (1989): 14, 15, www.cbeinternational.org/resource/article/priscilla-papers-academic-journal/beginning-beginning.

[36]Hiebert, "Beginning at the Beginning," 15.

[37]Hiebert, "Beginning at the Beginning," 15-16.

[38]Hiebert, "Beginning at the Beginning," 15.

[39]Hiebert, "Beginning at the Beginning," 16.

the messages of gender disparity and replacing them with the message that each of us is called to use the best of our abilities so we can go wherever that takes us. This will require a critical examination of the messages we have received throughout our lives and those we pass along to others. It will also require a commitment to freeing ourselves from the restrictions they impose. These will be the focus of the last half of this book.

But first, we will examine how the many forms of implicit socialization culminate in the very different experiences of two individuals, Sarah and Michael, as they discern and respond to God's call.

RECOMMENDED READING

Grady, J. Lee. *10 Lies the Church Tells Women: How the Bible Has Been Misused to Keep Women in Spiritual Bondage*. Lake Mary, FL: Charisma House, 2000.

Stouffer, Austin H. *95 More for the Door: A Layperson's Biblical Guide to Today's Gender Reformation*. Winnipeg, MB: Word Alive, 2008.

Hiebert, Frances. "Beginning at the Beginning." *Priscilla Papers* 3, no. 3. Christians for Biblical Equality. www.cbeinternational.org/resource/article/priscilla-papers-academic-journal/beginning-beginning.

Cunningham, Carolyn M., Heather M. Crandall, and Alexa M. Dare, eds. *Gender, Communication, and the Leadership Gap*. Charlotte, NC: Information Age, 2017.

George, Janet. *Still Side by Side: A Concise Explanation of Biblical Equality*. Minneapolis: Christians for Biblical Equality, 2009.

Fleming, Bruce C. E., Joy Fleming, and Joanne Guarnieri Hagemeyer. *The Book of Eden, Genesis 2-3: God Didn't Curse Eve (or Adam) or Limit Woman in Any Way*. Think Again Publishers, 2021.

Calhoun, Adele Ahlberg, and Tracey D. Bianchi. *True You: Overcoming Self-Doubt and Using Your Voice*. Downers Grove, IL: InterVarsity Press, 2014.

4

TWO STORIES: SARAH AND MICHAEL

In this chapter we will consider how gendered socialization might shape the lives and occupational decisions of two fictional people: Sarah and Michael.

SARAH'S STORY

Sarah was born into a healthy family. Her parents loved her, disciplined her with firm sensitivity, and made every decision with her best interest in mind. They took her to church, read to her, and played with her. They appropriately monitored the television and movies she watched, the games she played, and the people with whom she spent time.

By her first birthday, she had received twenty dolls from parents and grandparents, extended family, and friends. She also had a kitchen set, toy dishes, a play vacuum cleaner, and a shelf full of books telling her about stranger danger and how to be a good little girl. She loved playing dress-up and riding her pink tricycle with Barbie's picture on the seat.

Her parents readily played with her, and although her dad would roughhouse some, her mom would usually remind him to be careful. "She's just a little girl," she would say. Play dates with other girls often included tea parties where good manners were practiced. Sometimes they would fight over who got to be the mommy, but one of their mothers would always remind them to take turns and to use their inside voices.

When Sarah was five years old, she started school. She was bright, eager to learn, and always did her best to please the teachers. Except for Bs in math, she made straight As. Her teacher spoke with her mother about it. She reminded her that Sarah was bright, but math was harder for girls and not to be alarmed. "Math was never my best subject either," her mother replied. But not to worry, they would see if Sarah's father could help on days he got home early enough. Sarah's grade went up after that, and her parents praised her for working so hard.

Her parents taught Sarah to pick up her toys and make her bed each morning. She also set the table and helped her mother wash and dry the dishes. As she got older, she helped dust and vacuum and learned to prepare some foods on her own. When her younger cousin came over, she would keep him occupied so the adults could visit. But once when she let him play with her dolls and dishes, his parents reminded her he might prefer the plastic ball and bat in the back of her closet.

She had lots of friends and loved making up games to play when they came over. She would get annoyed, though, when they wouldn't listen to her explain the rules. Then one time her mom pulled her aside and told her to quit being so bossy. Bossy? She was just trying to teach them how to play the game. After a while she learned to give instructions differently. Instead of just saying "Do this," she would look confused and say, "Hmm . . . maybe if we did it this way?" when she knew good and well how to do it. I mean, she invented the game! But whatever. When she said it like that, her friends didn't get mad, and her mom quit telling her to "play nice."

In her free time, Sarah loved to read. She loved biographies about people who did extraordinary things. She read about inventors like the Wright brothers and adventurers like Daniel Boone, Neil Armstrong, and Amelia Earhart. She read about people who changed the world, like Abraham Lincoln, Martin Luther King, and Clara Barton.

For a while she thought about doing something extraordinary herself when she grew up. She was confused, though, since most of the biographies she read were of men. That might have been a coincidence. But then one biography had a section on becoming an inventor. The first sentence said, "If a person wants to invent something useful, he should learn all he can about science." He? Well, what did that mean? Could she be an inventor too? Or was that just for boys?

Maybe it's like at church when we sing that song about "sinful men." Her mom had explained that it meant sinful people, not just men. And that Bible verse about becoming "sons of God," that was really about children of God, her Sunday school teacher said. But when the pastor got up and resigned last Sunday, he said they should pray for the next pastor to be God's man. She asked her dad if that meant man or woman. Her dad said no, it had to be a man.

It was confusing. When did "he" and "man" mean everyone, and when did they just mean "he" and "man"?

When Sarah got to middle school, things changed. Her body, for one. Sometimes she heard boys say things as she walked down the hall. It made her uncomfortable, like maybe she had done something wrong. She tried to act like she didn't hear them or if it was obvious she did, she would just smile and blink rather than respond. Maybe if she didn't make a fuss, they would quit. Once it almost made her cry, and she told one of her teachers. But the teacher just shook her head and smiled. "Boys will be boys," she had said.

So, I guess it's normal? Sarah assumed it was since no one made them stop.

Not all boys were gross, though. One in her algebra class was really cute. Sarah had read an article about how to talk to boys. It said not to worry if you had pimples or didn't have the perfect body, but all the magazines had pictures on the cover of skinny girls who were otherwise well developed, with perfect skin and hair. So, did it matter or didn't it?

One article said boys notice you more if you wear makeup, so she did. And if you don't talk too much, so she tried that too. When the teacher would call on her to explain how she had solved an algebra equation, Sarah would sit there and shrug. No sense making him think she was a showoff, not if she wanted him to like her. Once when they got tests back, he asked how she had done. She saw the A on the top of his paper. So, she gave him a sad smile and showed him the B at the top of hers. He said not to worry; they could study together for the next test. After that, she didn't mind the Bs so much.

Once she got to high school, her parents, teachers, and guidance counselor talked a lot about college. She had always known she would go, and her parents expected it, but she didn't know for sure what she should take when she got there. Maybe she would be a secretary like her mom or a teacher like her aunt. She especially liked the idea of teaching children because she had a lot of experience babysitting. Plus, summers off would be good once she had children.

But she prayed a lot and lately felt like she should work in the church. But what could she do? Boys were pastors; girls were—what?—pastor's wives, she guessed. But what if she didn't meet a boy she liked who wanted to be a pastor? Should she just teach Sunday school or volunteer for the nursery a lot? She didn't know, but it didn't seem like enough somehow. Her teachers told her she was a gifted speaker and an excellent writer, but other than preaching, how could she use those skills at church?

As she neared the end of high school, she had a boyfriend and decided not to make too big a deal about what to major in when she got to college. It probably wouldn't matter. When they got married, she would have to see what he wanted to do and where he could find a job. And when they had kids, she wouldn't be able to focus on a career anyway.

Plus, she had read a book her youth leader recommended that was all about relationships with guys. The writer said respect was more important for men than for women. It was hard-wired even. And for her to have a good marriage one day, she would have to show him lots of respect. It would be hard, she supposed, but she wanted to do the right thing, and her Sunday school teacher had done a whole series last year about the importance of service and putting others first the way Christ had done for the church. It was a little confusing, though, because the boys' class had covered another book series about being good leaders because Christ had led his disciples well. She wondered why they never got around to that series in the girls' class.

At the end of high school, however, she and her boyfriend broke up. She went to college, where she majored in English and decided to be a writer. She might teach. Then, once she had children, she could stay home with them and write the Great American Novel. And if she still wanted to contribute to the church, she could always write devotionals or Sunday school curricula, especially for children. Her denomination would surely allow that. She didn't understand it completely, but her parents believed what the church taught and so many people smarter than she seemed to agree.

When she got to college, things changed again. One of her professors encouraged her to submit an essay to a writing competition. She didn't think she would win but wanted to please the professor, who really wanted her to enter. Much to her surprise, she did win! She also got involved in a campus organization that went out to community churches on Sundays to lead Bible study and worship. Once they asked her to fill in for a student who was sick and couldn't preach. She was terrified but didn't want the church to be without someone, so she agreed. Everyone told her how well she had done. And it felt good! Still, she had qualms about girls preaching, so she didn't do it again.

At least, not until after a course in gender studies. Her professor said each person—male and female—should serve as God chose to use them. From the class discussions and readings, along with prayer and Bible study, she decided women could lead, preach, pastor and whatever else God called them to do. She began to pray for discernment for her own calling. Soon after, she added a biblical studies major and planned for seminary after graduation. Sarah would become a pastor. She couldn't wait to use her gifts for God and the church.

Her senior year, she met and began dating James. He was a political science major and planned to go to law school after graduation. Did he object to having a preacher wife? No, he vowed support for whatever she wanted to do.

It might be difficult, though, for them to be students at the same time. They needed money to live on. So, he suggested they take turns. Although she had hoped to begin graduate school immediately after college, he felt strongly that he should go first. His family had invested a lot financially in his career and had always pushed him to succeed. He had such natural ability, would graduate with honors, and was already accepted into a prestigious law school. He just couldn't disappoint them. They wouldn't understand. After all, he argued, did it really matter who went first as long as they each reached their goals?

Sarah supposed not. She could wait. She wanted to be a good wife, and good wives supported their husbands. It wasn't worth fighting over. Plus, he was already more supportive of her than any of her friends' husbands. Wouldn't it be silly to make an issue of something this petty? So, she agreed he would go first. She would work to support them as he completed law school, then he would work while she attended seminary. It would be fine.

She felt good about the decision. James was happy. So were his parents. Her parents were happy too. They liked James and his ambition. "Besides," they said, "being married to a lawyer, you won't ever really have to work." They quickly added, "Oh, we know you want to," they winked, "but you never know how many children the Lord will give you."

So, she served on a church staff as a children's minister. Her family was happy she could follow her call while James was in school. Of course, children's ministry wasn't actually her call, but they were so happy, as was James, that she didn't correct them.

As he finished law school, however, he had a shot at a position with a highly respected firm that would provide great opportunities for him down the line. He was so excited to be considered and insisted that he interview with them. "Just for the experience," he said. She was happy for him, but she didn't see the point of an interview since he couldn't accept the job if they made him an offer. It was two hundred miles away, and there were no schools in the area where she could pursue her degree. She reminded him that her education was the next priority. He agreed but seemed hurt.

She felt horrible standing in his way like that. And maybe they should at least consider it. God could work through anything, right? *If he gets the job, maybe that's a sign we're supposed to move*, she thought. Two of her close friends just had babies, and they asked when she would have one. Her mother reminded her she wasn't getting any younger. And truthfully, she would love to have a child soon.

Maybe that's what this was about. Maybe God wanted her to focus on family right now. James could take the job, they could pay some bills, and they could have a child. She could still work part-time, or even volunteer, at a church wherever they lived. And who said she had to pastor? Maybe she just needed to serve God where she could. Anyway, isn't ministry about service instead of vying for leadership?

He interviewed, and they offered him the position. She resigned from her job, and they moved. Shortly after, they had their first baby, then a second. James continued to receive accolades at work, and Sarah was very proud of him. She loved being a mom and making James's parents and her own so happy.

Somehow, pastoring didn't seem as important as it once did.

At least that's what she told herself. But any time a young person at church spoke of being called to ministry, she felt a surge of longing. She would think about the dreams she once had and those who encouraged her along the way—the English professor who entered her essay into that competition, her gender studies professor who believed God could use women, her Bible professor who encouraged her to pursue a seminary education and the pastorate.

She didn't know if they were right or not. It seemed so long ago.

Then one day, their church brought in a candidate they hoped would become their new pastor. This woman spoke to the congregation about her call to ministry and the obstacles she had faced along the way. The obstacles sounded all too familiar to Sarah. *I used to want to be a minister*, she thought wistfully. *What happened? How did I get here?*

A part of herself had died. Was it too late to get it back?

MICHAEL'S STORY

Michael was born to parents who were thrilled to have a son. They loved him, gave him plenty of affection, and disciplined him with firmness and love. They monitored his friendships, television, games, and social media in age-appropriate ways. They took him to church, helped him with homework, and encouraged him in his interests.

For birthdays and Christmas, Michael was given sports equipment, race cars, and computer games. Some gifts were rougher than his mother liked, but his dad told her it was all harmless. "Boys will be boys," he would say. Michael and his dad spent a lot of time outside playing catch or riding the four-wheeler around their property. They would come in laughing and dirty, and his mother would "tut tut" about the noise and the mess. She was so happy they spent time together; she never asked him to clean it up. She would do it.

But he did help around the house. When he was little, he had to pick up his toys and make his bed each morning. When he was older, he took out the garbage and mowed the grass in the summer. He learned to paint when his parents remodeled and got pretty good with motors, too, when his dad let him help.

Michael read a lot for fun, mostly books about boys who became superheroes or wizards, or biographies about men who achieved great things. His favorites were sports heroes and people who made lots of money, like Bill Gates. He wanted to do something big enough to have his own biography written one day. His parents told him he could if he wanted. He was certainly smart enough.

And he was smart. Always had been. Except for the Bs in math, he brought home As in everything. Once in a while, his teacher would playfully reprimand him, suggesting he buckle down and get serious so his math grade would reflect his ability. Once when his parents talked to his teacher about it, she told them not to worry; he was just more interested in playing than studying. Once he determined to give it his best effort, it would all fall into place, she had said. Michael's parents chuckled because that's what they thought too. That's the way it is with boys who are smart. They all agreed.

Michael's parents were churchgoers, and they instilled in him a love of God and desire to help those in need. They attended church on Sunday, and he was a faithful member of a Sunday school class and the youth group when he got old enough. The youth leader always presented relevant topics for discussion, which Michael found interesting. They read books on becoming fearless men of God and how the church has tried to make men more like women, but that being God's warrior was their rightful place. Twice he was asked to preach on youth Sunday. He appreciated all the comments he received, especially when several people told him he was better than their regular preacher!

He began to wonder if he might be called to pastor. He mentioned it to his parents and youth leader, who promised to pray for him in this decision and gave him more books to read on being God's man in the world.

Church was a good place for Michael. He didn't understand it when others felt differently. One Sunday evening a lady spoke about how the church hadn't been as welcoming to women as it should be. Something about not believing their experiences and the language of the church not being inclusive. He looked through the hymnal and, sure enough, there were more songs that spoke of men than women. And their pastor did preach more on David and Paul than Ruth and Phoebe.

He agreed it must be tough for girls. But he couldn't see that complaining would help any. Maybe they should just worry less about being equal and look for ways to serve. That's what he did; he never tried to take power from the women's mission group or demand to be part of the girls' Bible study on Wednesday nights. He just looked for ways to get involved; he preached occasionally and represented the youth on the pastor search committee.

He meant to ask his girlfriend what she thought, but he never got around to it. He had college applications to fill out and between his parents and pastor he felt a lot of pressure to get it done early. While he still wanted to go into ministry, his school guidance counselor told him to consider other options too. He had the highest ACT score of any student in his class and had a good shot at an Ivy League school. She suggested that he consider pre-med.

Although he planned to be a minister, being a doctor appealed to him. Sure, it would be hard work, but then it would pay off big time. He could help sick people, maybe find the cure for something. He would have money and status, and his family could live in a huge house.

But then again, he'd be a good preacher too. And his girlfriend would be a great pastor's wife, just like the wife of their current pastor. She had put him through seminary and was really nice. Plus, she worked as hard as her husband at the church and never seemed to mind at all. Everyone joked that the church got two for the price of one.

Once Michael got to college, he worked hard and kept his grades up. His academic adviser helped him process his thoughts about ministry versus medicine and helped him decide on ministry as his life's work. His adviser helped him find money for seminary and talked with him extensively about the best way to meet the needs of a congregation without getting burned out. "And be careful who you marry," his adviser told him. "Make sure she understands and supports you in your call. She will have to understand God comes first, so hopefully she won't try to pull you away from this important work God has called you to."

He knew he had nothing to worry about with his girlfriend, Jennifer. And he was right. They got married after he graduated from college. She worked to support him while he was in seminary and understood that his studies had to come first, since he was a man of God and everything.

And it wasn't like he didn't sacrifice too. He would love to spend more time with her and the baby, but between school and the church he pastored, he didn't have much time at home. Yes, sacrifice was a two-way street.

After seminary, he was called to a full-time pastorate. Now his wife could quit her job. She didn't mind since she only had it to keep them afloat financially. She could stay home and take care of their child and the second one who would be born in a few months. He was glad to make it easier on her. This way she could focus on him and the children without the stress of a job.

He had struggled through school and sacrificed a lot, but it had finally paid off.

For everyone.

RECOMMENDED READING

Hansen, Jodi, and David Hansen. "When Gender Roles Don't Work: How One Couple and Their Sons Became Egalitarians." CBE Blog/Magazine. September 4, 2018. www.cbeinternational.org/resource/article/mutuality-blog-magazine/when-gender-roles-dont-work-how-one-couple-and-their-sons.

Henderson, Heather. "My First Time: When Being Who God Made You Isn't Okay." CBE Blog/Magazine. March 4, 2018. www.cbeinternational.org/resource/article/mutuality-blog-magazine/my-first-time-when-being-who-god-made-you-isnt-okay.

Lindsay, Sarah. "She Leads with Confidence: Profile of a Pastor at Midlife." CBE Blog/Magazine. December 7, 2020. www.cbeinternational.org/resource/article/mutuality-blog-magazine/she-leads-confidence-profile-pastor-midlife.

Thao, Touger. "Paying Attention to Fatherhood: Why I Stepped Down from Pastoral Ministry." CBE Blog/Magazine. March 4, 2017. www.cbeinternational.org/resource/article/mutuality-blog-magazine/paying-attention-fatherhood-why-i-stepped-down-pastoral.

Westbrook, Sierra Neiman. "Choose Your Own Adventure: A Very Egalitarian Proposal." CBE Blog/Magazine. March 3, 2019. www.cbeinternational.org/resource/article/mutuality-blog-magazine/choose-your-own-adventure-very-egalitarian-proposal.

5 CREATING MORE ACCURATE SELF-PERCEPTIONS

In the first few chapters of this book, I provided an overview of the implicit messages girls and women receive that channel them away from leadership. Since you are still reading, this material likely resonated with you. You probably identified messages that encouraged you toward some pursuits and away from others and identified decisions you made based on those messages.

I want to reiterate that this information has not been presented to place blame on those who nurtured us. Parents generally have the best of intentions—to raise responsible, good human beings. Likewise, religious leaders typically strive to impart truths that will help us to live well. I have nothing but respect for my own parents, teachers, and pastors who shaped me and provided my religious training. Rather, critically examining what they taught us is an important step in completing the work they started—to become responsible adults able to discern truth that we may live well.

Therefore, in the remaining chapters, we will explore ways you can make changes within yourself and within your sphere of influence. Specifically, in this chapter you will learn to assess the accuracy of messages you have received and explore ways to build more accurate self-perceptions so you are freer to answer God's call.

MESSAGES CREATE A MENTAL FRAMEWORK

We will begin by exploring the mindset, the "mental attitude or inclination," created by subtle and consistent messages.[1] As I have said, these messages are especially powerful since we usually don't even notice them, much less make an effort to fend them off. If someone explicitly told me that I could not have a certain job because I'm a woman, I would immediately identify their flawed reasoning and counter their argument. If this were for a job in ministry, I might ask them to share the Scripture on which they base their position, and I could then share my interpretation of the same. If this were in a secular setting, I would research the laws about sex discrimination in the workplace and fight for my rights. However, when messages are indirect and subtle—implicit—we often don't recognize them until we are well into adulthood. By then, they have shaped many of our decisions without our knowing what or how it happened.

A friend of mine went on several weekend ministry teams as a college student and was a member of her campus's Fellowship of Christian Athletes and Baptist Student Union. It wasn't until talking with me about this book—some twenty years after her graduation—that it occurred to her that a female student never spoke on the weekend teams, and neither organization was led by a woman. When messages are unspoken and indirect, we often do not notice what they communicate until much later.

These messages gain power when they come consistently from a variety of sources. We see male CEOs with secretaries who are women. Our pastors and deacons are men, while women serve as children's leaders or head up the kitchen committee. The education system chimes in with its assessment of our potential. And when Dad is referred to as head of the family or his opinion

---

[1]*Merriam-Webster Dictionary*, s.v. "mindset," www.merriam-webster.com/dictionary/mindset.

weighs in more heavily than Mom's, this message is solidified as truth.

These consistent messages create a mental framework through which we decide what is and is not appropriate for us to do. It nudges us toward some jobs, away from others. It prompts us to second guess whether we should apply for that promotion or remain free to go part-time when household demands increase.

Then when anyone asks why we never followed through with the ambitious dreams of our youth, we might not be able to give a compelling reason. "It just never felt right," we respond. We don't know why. Maybe we weren't called to anything more than what we're doing now, we conclude.

I hope this book has presented you with another explanation and challenged you to restructure your own mental framework. This time based on truth.

DISCERNING TRUTH: FOLLOW THE EVIDENCE

But discerning truth isn't always easy. Messages often come to us as children before we are capable of thinking critically about their accuracy. In 1 Corinthians 13:11, Paul states, "When I was a child, I spoke like a child, I thought like a child, I reasoned like a child; when I became an adult, I put an end to childish ways" (NRSV). His words are echoed by developmentalists who remind us that we can't expect children to think and reason as they will later once the brain has fully developed. In the same way, we can't expect the child we once were to have adequately sorted through the barrage of messages she was given and select only the ones that were accurate.

But as adults we can expect just that. We can treat the messages we've been given as we would information from any other source: by examining the evidence to discern its accuracy, to determine which messages to keep and which to eliminate.

Consider past experiences. For instance, if you were told as a child that you were shy and would have stage fright if you got up to speak in front of others, you might have believed it without question. Your mindset told you then, and continues to tell you now, that if you speak in public, you will surely die (or at least pass out, throw up, whatever). So, as an adult, when given the opportunity to preach a sermon, present your research at a professional conference, or speak to potential donors for your organization, your mindset warns you about your stage fright. You are tempted to forgo the opportunity.

But before you do, I ask that you look for the evidence. Ask yourself, *In the past when I spoke in front of others, did my prediction come true? Did I, in fact, die or pass out, stumble over my words, trip as I walked into the room? Did people laugh at me or throw tomatoes*? If not, then you have evidence to the contrary.

You might also consider where you first heard the message. Was it from an adult who had stage fright? Well-meaning though she was, did she project her fears onto you? If so, reexamining the initial situation with an adult mind can counter inaccuracy with truth.

Listen to others' assessments. Listen to those who compliment you. That can be difficult as we often dismiss what others say as friends just being nice. But if you hear it consistently, consider that their words might be accurate.

During the first part of my teaching career, I envied colleagues who easily interacted with students outside of class. They would invite students into their homes for a meal, sponsor trips to conference locations, or lead student groups at church. Other faculty encouraged me to do the same.

But I wouldn't. I didn't think I had the personality to pull it off. On the rare occasion when I did host an event, I would ask another colleague to join us to provide a buffer of sorts to ease my discomfort.

Afterward, the students and colleagues alike assured me of the fun and good food I had provided. I should do it more often, they would say. But I told myself they were just being nice.

Then one semester while preparing to speak at a conference, one of my students expressed interest in getting more involved in professional organizations. I obtained the funding for her to attend, and to cut her expenses I invited her to ride the eight-hour journey across three states with my family and me. During the travel time and conference weekend, she and I spent a lot of time together. We discussed what we were learning in the sessions we attended. We talked about her plans for graduate school. We got lost in this unfamiliar city late one night and only found our way back through trial and error and a lot of laughter. As the trip ended, I thanked her for going with us, as if she had only gone under duress. "Why wouldn't I want to go?" she asked. She seemed genuinely perplexed. She had had a wonderful time. My mental framework began to shift.

Soon after, a student who often came by my office asked if we could have an end-of-the-semester get-together at my house. He wouldn't be returning the next semester and wanted to have one last evening with several other students he had met in my classes. I happily complied and made pasta for this small group. We spent the evening eating, playing games, and talking about summer plans. After they left—rather late into the evening—I realized what had happened: a student with limited time on campus had *asked* to come to my house. When other students heard the plan, they happily joined us. No one had been in a rush to leave. What's more, I hadn't invited another colleague to be my buffer.

I expressed to a friend my amazement at the good time everyone seemed to have. She was puzzled. "You're the only one who's surprised at this," she said. And I was. Even with much evidence to the contrary, I was still clinging to an inaccurate mindset.

Now, roughly six years later, the conference and the finals week gathering have become regular events. The students from that group have graduated, but new ones join us each semester to fill the seats around the table. Often, former students will even return to catch up and meet their "successors." I am happy to report that they still enjoy themselves. One thing, however, has changed: whereas I doubted myself before, I now know I can do this. Thankfully, I began to listen to the spoken and unspoken messages that were being sent my way—messages that spoke truth to an inaccurate mindset and freed me to be the mentor I am called to be.

What about you? Are you consistently told that you are good at mediating others' disputes? Then your mindset is inaccurate when it says you aren't good with people. Do others come to you for wisdom and guidance? Then don't believe it when your mindset says you are not insightful enough to lead. Do others say you are a good communicator and a source of encouragement? Then don't accept the mental framework that insists you won't be able to preach a sermon that inspires.

Ask those you trust. Find someone who knows you well enough to give you a fair appraisal and someone honest enough to do so. Share your concerns and ask for their insight. Ask more than one person if possible. Even those who know us well might have different perspectives; you'll want to take them all into account. And those that are consistent? Give them serious consideration.

Are you persuasive enough to be a motivational speaker? Will you be able to deal with the additional workload a promotion would bring? Do you have the organizational skills to go back to school while managing a household?

Don't know? Ask. Several people.

And listen to their answers.

THE COGNITIVE-BEHAVIORAL APPROACH TO CHANGE

Once you have identified your inaccurate misperceptions, you are ready to make some changes. Before we cover specific techniques, however, let's explore some basics of behavior change.

Psychologists often conceptualize behavior as being composed of three components: overt behavior, cognitions, and affect. These components are interrelated, with a change in one often prompting a change in the others. For instance, in the example above, when I began believing (cognition) that I was capable of successfully hosting students in my home, I was more inclined to do so (overt behavior), which in turn bolstered my thoughts (cognitions) about myself as a capable host and fostered increased confidence (affect) in my ability to interact effectively with students outside of class. A shift in one part of the system led to a shift in the others (see figure 5.1).

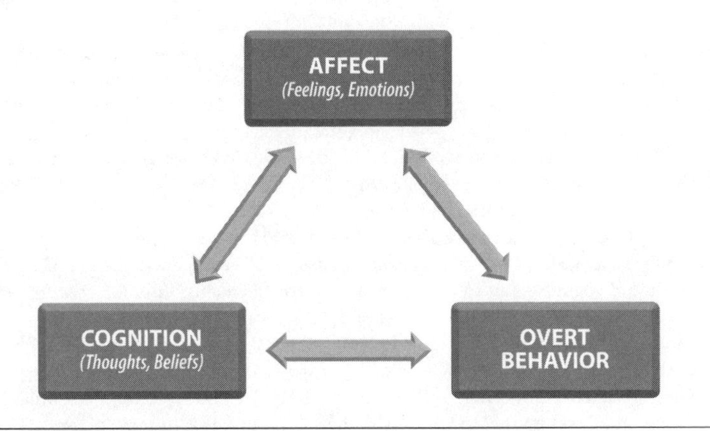

Figure 5.1. Interaction between affect, cognition, and overt behavior

The interrelatedness of these components is supported extensively by research. Cognitive therapy utilizes a systematic restructuring of cognitions to prompt behavior change. Cognitive-behavioral therapy

(CBT) does the same by targeting overt behaviors along with cognitions. Both are well-established treatments for disorders of affect such as depression and anxiety.[2] CBT has also been identified as holding promise for the treatment of insomnia and eating disorders.[3]

In addition, the ABC-X Model of family therapy suggests that the interpretation (cognition) assigned to an event is one determinant of whether the event will result in a crisis (overt behavior and affect) for the family and its members.[4] For instance, Dad's job loss could be interpreted as his failure to provide. But it might also be interpreted as an opportunity for him to explore more satisfying job opportunities. Seeing this event as an opportunity rather than a failure

---

[2]For information on the use of cognitive and cognitive-behavioral treatments for depression, see Valerie Gloaguen et al., "A Meta-Analysis of the Effects of Cognitive Therapy in Depressed Patients," *Journal of Affective Disorders* 49 (1998): 59; Keith S. Dobson, "A Meta-Analysis of the Efficacy of Cognitive Therapy for Depression," *Journal of Consulting and Clinical Psychology* 57, no. 3 (1989): 414; Sarah E. Watts et al., "Treatment-as-Usual (TAU) Is Anything but Usual: A Meta-Analysis of CBT Versus TAU for Anxiety and Depression," *Journal of Affective Disorders* 175 (2015): 152, https://doi.org/10.1016/j.jad.2014.12.025; Mina Honyashiki et al., "Specificity of CBT for Depression: A Contribution from Multiple Treatments Meta-Analyses," *Cognitive Therapy Research* 38 (2014): 249, https://doi.org/10.1007/s10608-014-9599-7; and Serap Keles and Thormod Idsoe, "A Meta-Analysis of Group Cognitive-Behavioral Therapy (CBT) Interventions for Adolescents with Depression," *Journal of Adolescence* 67 (2018): 129, https://doi.org/10.1016/j.adolescence.2018.05.011. For information on the use of cognitive and cognitive-behavioral treatments for anxiety, see Jedidiah Siev and Dianne L. Chambless, "Specificity of Treatment Effects: Cognitive Therapy and Relaxation for Generalized Anxiety and Panic Disorders," *Journal of Consulting and Clinical Psychology* 75, no. 4 (2007): 513, https://doi.org/10.1037/0022-006X.75.4.513; Dianne L. Chambless and Martha M. Gillis, "Cognitive Therapy of Anxiety Disorders," *Journal of Consulting and Clinical Psychology* 61, no. 2 (1993): 248; and Watts et al., "Treatment-as-Usual," 152.

[3]For the use of cognitive and cognitive-behavioral treatments for insomnia, see Annemieke van Straten et al., "Cognitive and Behavioral Therapies in the Treatment of Insomnia: A Meta-Analysis," *Sleep Medicine Reviews* 38 (2018): 3. For the use of these treatments for eating disorders, see Eric Dumont et al., "A New Cognitive Behavior Therapy for Adolescents with Avoidant/Restrictive Food Intake Disorder in a Day Treatment Setting: A Clinical Case Series," *International Journal of Eating Disorders* 52 (2019): 447, https://doi.org/10.1002/eat.23053, and Davy Vancampfort et al., "Changes in Physical Activity, Physical Fitness, Self-Perception and Quality of Life Following a 6-Month Physical Activity Counseling and Cognitive Behavioral Therapy Program in Outpatients with Binge Eating Disorder," *Psychiatry Research* 219, no. 2 (2014): 361.

[4]Michael Rosino, "ABC-X Model of Family Stress and Coping," in *The Wiley Blackwell Encyclopedia of Family Studies*, ed. Constance L. Shehan (Malden, MA: John Wiley & Sons, 2016), https://doi.org/10.1002/9781119085621.wbefs313.

would be pivotal in the family's behavior toward Dad and for his motivation to move forward.

Scripture also supports the value of harnessing our thoughts to change behavior. Paul encouraged followers of Christ to "be transformed by the renewing of [the] mind" (Romans 12:2). In other words, we have the capacity to change our behavior by first changing our thoughts. Likewise, Paul states that we can enjoy the peace of God (affect) by first thinking on (cognition) "whatever is true, whatever is noble, whatever is right, whatever is pure, whatever is lovely, whatever is admirable" (Philippians 4:8).

While effective, the process isn't always easy. In 2 Corinthians 10:5, Paul tells us to "take captive every thought to make it obedient to Christ." The use of the word *captive* suggests that the process can be arduous. One of my therapist friends describes it like this: If you are in a room with someone who seeks to take you captive, the way for you to be free without fear of being overtaken would be to take that person captive yourself. A physical struggle would likely ensue as you each attempt to overpower the other, thereby ensuring your own freedom. At the finish you would be sweaty, out of breath, your heart pounding. This is the image she uses in preparing her clients for the process of taking their own thoughts captive. It won't be easy, she tells them. They will fight for the freedom they seek. But it will be worth it in the end. In the same way, we can expect that some of the thoughts we must replace will be difficult to overtake. We will have to work hard to get the best of them. The struggle might take a while, but it will be worth it when we are free.

Cognitions do not have to be the starting point, however. We can also begin the process by first changing our overt behavior and subsequently experience a change in our thoughts and feelings. For example, those who teach study skills often advise unmotivated students to commit to spending ten minutes on homework assignments.

Once they spend even that short amount of time on task, they build momentum, motivation follows, and they continue working on the assignment for a much longer period of time.

And since we improve on the skills we practice, spending time on homework increases our understanding of the subject, which also fuels motivation. Scripture also supports the effect that behavior has on thoughts and feelings. Jesus said to forgive "not seven times, but seventy-seven times" (Matthew 18:22). If practice makes perfect, the consistent practice of forgiveness would make forgiveness come more easily across time.

But social psychologists tell us it is more than momentum or that practice makes perfect. Rather, when our behavior is in opposition to our thoughts, we attempt to resolve this *cognitive dissonance* by modifying our thoughts to make them consistent with our behavior. Those who appreciate others often credit their parents, who expected them, as children, to smile and express gratitude when receiving a gift. On a societal scale, prejudice against minorities decreased when laws against racial and gender discrimination in the workplace were enacted and enforced. In other words, "fake it till you make it" is supported by science.

In their book *Psychology Through the Eyes of Faith*, David G. Myers and Malcolm A. Jeeves assert that the Bible supports the inter-relationship of feelings and obedient action.[5] They maintain that "throughout the Old and New Testaments we are told that full knowledge of God comes through actively doing the Word" and that "faith is nurtured by obedience."[6]

The fact that we can initiate change from more than one point in the system—with cognitions or with behavior—means we have a

[5]David G. Myers and Malcolm A. Jeeves, *Psychology Through the Eyes of Faith*, rev. and updated (New York: HarperCollins, 2003), 195.

[6]Myers and Jeeves, *Psychology Through the Eyes of Faith*, 195.

variety of tools in bringing about the change we seek. In the next section, we will explore both cognitive and behavioral techniques that can move you toward healthier self-perceptions and motivate you to fulfill your potential.

COGNITIVE TECHNIQUES

Positive self-talk. Research indicates the value of positive self-talk in modifying competence beliefs, lowering anxiety related to public speaking, and lowering competitive anxiety and increasing self-compassion.[7] It seems to restructure our thoughts in much the same way those earlier messages initially created our mental framework. You might use a verse of Scripture that encourages you, a quote from a book you've read, or a statement you've written yourself. Those most helpful for me encompass truths that I aspire to but which, so far, have been outside my grasp.

Recently I was asked to take on a project that I knew would bolster the quality of my writing but would consume more time than I had to offer. Feeling called to do something that I could not imagine doing well frightened me. Each morning while preparing for my day, I repeated the phrase, "I will have all the time I need to do this job well." While I didn't believe those words the first time I said them, I repeated them daily to open myself to truth. One day I realized that I no longer doubted those words.

[7]For information on the use of positive self-talk in modifying competence beliefs, see Sander Thomaes et al., "Effort Self-Talk Benefits the Mathematics Performance of Children with Negative Competence Beliefs," *Child Development* 91, no. 6 (2019): 2211, https://doi.org/10.1111/cdev.13347. For information on the use of positive self-talk in public-speaking anxiety, see Xiaowei Shi, Thomas M. Brinthaupt, and Margaret McCree, "The Relationship of Self-Talk Frequency to Communication Apprehension and Public Speaking Anxiety," *Personality and Individual Differences* 75 (2015): 125, https://doi.org/10.1016/j.paid.2014.11.023. For information on the use of positive self-talk for competitive anxiety and self-compassion, see Styliani Kyriaki Georgakaki and Eirini Karakasidou, "The Effects of Motivational Self-Talk on Competitive Anxiety and Self-Compassion: A Brief Training Program Among Competitive Swimmers," *Scientific Research Publishing* 8, no. 5 (2017): 677, https://doi.org/10.4236/psych.2017.85044.

One thing I like about this technique is that it creates a constructive belief system rather than merely eliminating one that is faulty. A therapist friend of mine tells her clients that they must do more than merely eliminate old patterns of thinking. Stopping there would be like uprooting a tree and leaving a gaping hole in the ground—it will continue to trip you up on a regular basis. She tells them they must fill that hole with truth.

Positive self-talk can foster truth rather than simply eliminating the faulty thought pattern.

Reframing. How a picture is framed alters our perception of it. In the wrong frame, some aspects of a piece seem hidden, colors appear drab, leaving us void of an emotional response. When reframed, however, what appeared to be lackluster is shown to be a piece of art with the power to transform those who view it. Likewise, a reframe of our talents and abilities can transform our self-perception. Talents we hadn't noticed before come into view. Abilities that had seemed unremarkable now become vibrant. And our emotional response follows. In fact, reframing has long been used as a therapeutic technique.[8]

One way to do this is to put yourself in the following scenario. A woman of your own age comes to you for guidance. She has the abilities that you have and is gifted with the talents you possess. She is considering a change, one to which she is called and one which will utilize her abilities more fully than anything she has done so far. There will be a learning curve as she develops the specific skills she needs to step into this new endeavor. She will have to practice new behaviors and enlist the help of those closest to her. She will be very

---

[8]Denise C. Marigold, John G. Holmes, and Michael Ross, "More Than Words: Reframing Compliments from Romantic Partners Fosters Security in Low Self-Esteem Individuals," *Journal of Personality and Social Psychology* 92, no. 2 (2007): 232, https://doi.org/10.1037/0022-3514.92.2.232, and Daniel J. Pesut, "The Art, Science, and Techniques of Reframing in Psychiatric Mental Health Nursing," *Issues in Mental Health Nursing* 12, no. 1 (1991): 9, https://doi.org/10.3109/01612849109058206.

uncomfortable as she stretches herself in new ways. "What do you think?" she asks. "Should I go for it?"

What do you tell her? Possibly, "No, don't change a thing. The fulfillment of accepting God's call will never outweigh the difficulty of change. Your inner circle won't want to adjust their lives as you've adjusted for theirs. Don't do it."

I hope not.

I hope you would encourage her to trust herself if she believes this change is right. That she is up to the task. That those whom she will depend on have a responsibility to support her as she has supported them over the years.

We are often more encouraging of others than we are of ourselves. If you would encourage another person to experience the fullness of their abilities and talents, why not offer the same to yourself?

Mental imagery. In their article "Imagining Stereotypes Away," Irene V. Blair and her colleagues describe an exercise wherein they asked research participants to "imagine what a strong woman is like, why she is considered strong, what she is capable of doing, and what kinds of hobbies and activities she enjoys."[9] Among their participants, compared to a control group, there was a reduction of the implicit stereotype of women being weak.[10] Rather than simply telling people not to stereotype, they conclude that a more effective strategy would be to "encourage people to consider the diversity within social groups and especially [those] who disconfirm the stereotype."[11]

While this exercise lends itself to program implementation, individuals could use it as easily. For instance, to spend a few minutes

[9]Irene V. Blair, Jennifer E. Ma, and Alison P. Lenton, "Imagining Stereotypes Away: The Moderation of Implicit Stereotypes Through Mental Imagery," *Journal of Personality and Social Psychology* 81, no. 5 (2001): 830, https://doi.org/10.1037//0022-3514.81.5.828.

[10]Blair et al., "Imagining Stereotypes Away," 837.

[11]Blair et al., "Imagining Stereotypes Away," 838.

each day contemplating women who do things that run counter to gender stereotypes would be an effective means of achieving a less restricted view of women in general and of ourselves in particular.

And the more we are exposed to women who break stereotypes, the more salient these images become. Toward that end, you might specifically ask women you know to tell you their stories of success, of obstacles they have overcome, and how they did so. Even women you do not know as well—maybe a leader in your community or an accomplished woman at your church—might welcome the opportunity to share their stories with someone actively working on her own personal and professional growth.

For an even broader perspective, you can read books, articles, and news stories about accomplished women who have pushed past stereotypes in a diverse range of endeavors. Doing so might just transform your implicit views on what we, as women, can do and where we should do it.

Another way to utilize mental imagery is to consider what therapists refer to as the *inner child*.[12] While the childhood version of ourselves is present in each of us, in many, this child holds an abundance of restrictive messages that continue to limit us into adulthood. One way of using this technique is to speak to that child. As the receptacle of past messages—both accurate and inaccurate—to hear your reassurance of her worth and the correct versions of those faulty messages can heal her and move the person you are now in a healthier direction.

[12]Margareta Sjoblom et al., "From 9 to 91: Health Promotion Through the Life-Course—Illuminating the Inner Child," *Health Promotion International*, 2020, 6, https://doi.org/10.1093/heapro/daaa132; Athena Androutsopoulou and Maria Viou, "The Guided Imagery Therapy Activity 'Inner Dialogue-Child Adult Meeting' (ID-CAM): Steps and Applications," *Journal of Creativity in Mental Health* 14, no. 3 (2019): 343, https://doi.org/10.1080/15401383.2019.1624993; Asser Mikkel Hestbech, "Reclaiming the Inner Child in Cognitive-Behavioral Therapy: The Complementary Model of the Personality," *American Journal of Psychotherapy* 71, no. 1 (2018): 21; and Jeffery Smith, *Psychotherapy: A Practical Guide* (New York: Springer, 2017), 141.

One of my friends, when filled with self-doubt, imagines himself singing love songs to the child he once was—the child who, while free-spirited and innocent, was also frightened and felt alone. As he sings to this child, he finds himself comforted by this younger version of himself. He states that after one such experience, "I found myself fighting for him in a way that I often find hard to fight for this current version of me." He then tells that little boy, "I will be your biggest cheerleader for as long as you need, and it will be my life's mission to give you the life you deserve."

Most of us would fight tirelessly for our own children if we thought they were buying into lies that would hold them back. Can we also harness the strength to fight for our inner child when we are too tired to fight for ourselves?

BEHAVIORAL TECHNIQUES

Decide to seek and believe truth. Forgiveness researcher and author Everett Worthington makes a distinction between decisional and emotional forgiveness. Decisional forgiveness is a "behavioral intention statement . . . to behave toward the transgressor like one did prior to the transgression."[13] By itself, decisional forgiveness does not require that one *feel* forgiving, but is an act of will that might emerge from one's belief system. Worthington does suggest, however, that this decisional component usually leads to emotional forgiveness, which "necessarily reduces unforgiving emotions" and sometimes results in more positive emotions toward the offender.[14]

Worthington's model would seem to apply as easily to nurturing a more accurate mindset. As such, the act of will would be the decision to believe truth—about oneself and one's abilities and potential. This decision would therefore be the first step in replacing

[13]Everett L. Worthington Jr., *Forgiveness and Reconciliation: Theory and Application* (New York: Routledge, 2006), 56.
[14]Worthington, *Forgiveness and Reconciliation*, 56, 59.

unhealthy, harmful messages with those that are accurate and more productive. The emotional component—self-confidence, enthusiasm for opportunities—while not always present at first, can follow.

Realizing that the emotional component of any behavior might very well be absent at first can provide hope that it will come in time and that lasting change is indeed a process. Accepting that the process can begin with nothing more than our statement of will, grounded in our belief system, can reassure us that we have the power to initiate this life-altering process.

Of course, deciding to believe truth dictates that we open ourselves to the source of truth. Prayerful reading of Scripture and other sources like the ones recommended at the end of this chapter make for a good beginning.

Behave as if. Another technique that begins with a change in behavior is to behave *as if* we already possess the mental framework and affect we are trying to develop. This means that we exhibit the same behavior we would if we believed in ourselves and felt as confident as we hope to one day. We don't wait until the mental framework is in place. We don't hold off until we feel confident. We behave *now* as if we already had both.

And how do we behave when we have confidence? We typically seek opportunities to use our skills and talents. When presented with a challenge, we meet it rather than backing away prematurely. If others suggest that we are incapable, we know better and carry on.

The first time we attempt this, we might not feel anything close to capable and confident. We might even feel like a phony. But as we continue, we improve our level of skill, and the behavior will feel less forced. We no longer feel as if we are playing a role; instead, it's as if we have found a part of ourselves we didn't know existed.

As an introvert, I feel uncomfortable the first day of any class in which I don't know many of the students. Seeing thirty pairs of eyes staring back at me is daunting, and I often would rather walk right past the classroom and just keep going. However, when I enter the room, I always behave as if I am completely at ease. I initiate a get-acquainted activity, learn students' names, and make humorous observations as we discuss what the semester will entail. Before the hour is over, I find myself relaxed and enjoying myself with a group of people who are no longer strangers. When I behave as if I'm comfortable meeting students for the first time, I improve my interaction skills and thereby dispel that first-meeting anxiety introverts often experience.

Likewise, when we behave as if we are confident women following our call (e.g., accepting opportunities to use our gifts, speaking up when we have an idea, making direct statements instead of hedging), we hone our skills and increase our confidence accordingly.

Do the next right thing. Sometimes we can be hesitant to begin a journey if we don't see the entire path laid out for us in advance. We might decide to wait until we know exactly how we will get from point A to point B before we take the first step in behavior change. While the psalmist states, "Your word is a lamp for my feet, a light on my path" (Psalm 119:105), we are not guaranteed that the light will shine brightly over the entire path all at once. Some of the most helpful counsel I have received when doubting my next course of action is to *just do the next right thing.* Knowing the right thing for next week, next month, or next year isn't necessary in order to do the next right thing *today*.

As I write this chapter, our world is in the midst of a pandemic, requiring limited contact with others, masked social distancing, and a reconfiguration of how we conduct our work and personal interactions. In addition, the regular milestones and struggles of life—those unrelated to the pandemic—continue and require our attention. An elderly family member is diagnosed with a chronic illness. Graduations, birthdays, and holidays require creative ways of celebrating together while being apart. Several students I have mentored have graduated without the congratulatory sendoff I would have liked.

One day when feeling overwhelmed with how much I *cannot* do, I stopped to consider what I can do and what my next step should be in each of these situations. I can't host family during this health crisis, but we can still visit frequently by phone. A favorite holiday tradition can be modified and still work through social media. The graduation party won't happen, but I can express my pride in other ways.

Are any of these steps sufficient in themselves to solve the problems the pandemic has created? No. But for now, I just need to do the next right thing. So I call my mom. I rally my son and daughter, nieces and nephews for a new Christmas tradition. I mail a gift to the graduate. The light will shine on the next portion of the path before I get there.

Ask yourself what the next right thing is in your own journey. Could you agree to take on a task at work that will enhance your skill set? Might you put together your resume for when the next job opportunity arises? How about taking one class to test your comfort level as a college student?

Whatever the next right thing is—do it. The rest will follow.

THERAPY

While many dysfunctional thought patterns can be changed through exercises such as these, some require professional intervention. If you are unable to make the changes on your own, I encourage you to see a therapist. Sometimes when home or church environments are particularly restrictive, we are unable to recognize the patterns of behavior and thoughts that hold us back. Sometimes we recognize the problem but need more than can be provided in a book or through the exercises provided here. In these instances, a therapist who is trained in understanding thought patterns, emotional reactions, and behavior change can be an invaluable resource.

From years of referring others to mental health professionals, I know that some people are hesitant to consider therapy. While most people readily seek help from the medical community when suffering a physical malady, seeing a professional for emotional, mental, or behavior problems is more difficult for some. The fear of being seen as weak bothers a few. Concern for the expense and time involved holds some back. Others can't imagine how talking to "a stranger" could help.

Thankfully, as more people find help for mental health issues, the stigma continues to decline. Most therapists accept insurance, and some will work with you to make the process affordable. While a therapist who does their job well won't feel like a stranger for long, the fact that they *don't* know us from other contexts creates a safe space for us to learn and grow.

I have been a psychologist for several decades. During that time, I have been a professor, therapist, researcher, mentor, consultant, and writer. All the evidence attests to my being a relatively confident, informed, healthy individual. But I have still benefited several times over the years from therapists who helped me adjust my thought patterns, regulate my reaction to circumstances, and solidify behavior change. Therapy is for anyone who wants to be healthier and more effective in life. Whether your problems are driven by abuse, trauma, or just minor glitches in what you have learned along the way, therapy can be a resource in living a better life.

If you seek therapy, look for someone competent to do the work. You will see an array of titles, including psychologist, clinical social worker, mental health counselor, and marriage and family therapist. Regardless of the title, look for someone who is licensed to ensure that you are working with someone who has had ample training and supervised experience.

I often hear people say that they would see a therapist if they could find one who is a Christian. I understand that sharing similar beliefs with your therapist can be advantageous. I know several qualified Christian therapists and regularly make referrals to them. But one who is well trained should respectfully work within your frame of reference, regardless of their own personal beliefs. Their qualifications as a therapist should outweigh the fact that their religious beliefs align with your own. (Of course, if you seek spiritual guidance as well, you will indeed want to consider their religious beliefs and training along with their qualifications as a therapist.)

Regardless, however, make certain the person is egalitarian, believing that women and men are equal in value and rights. If your goal for therapy is to change a restrictive gendered mindset, the support of a therapist who shares your conviction will be essential to the process.

Most therapists will speak with you on the phone to answer questions before you set up a first meeting. It is appropriate for you to ask about their training, experience, and gender beliefs before you set up an appointment.

In conclusion, the process of restructuring one's mindset isn't easy. Changing a mental framework that we've built over decades is hard work. Sometimes we can make these changes by restructuring our thoughts or trying out behaviors that will move us in the right direction. Other times, a professional therapist is needed for lasting cognitive and behavior change.

We will move in that direction more quickly, however, when surrounded with others who have already developed, or are in the process of developing, a more accurate mindset themselves. Therefore, building a support system is crucial and is the topic of the next chapter.

RECOMMENDED READING

Leach, Tara Beth. *Emboldened: A Vision for Empowering Women in Ministry*. Downers Grove, IL: InterVarsity Press, 2017.

Martin, Nicole Massie. *Made to Lead: Empowering Women for Ministry*. Webster Groves, MO: Chalice, 2016.

Morgante, Camden. "How to Find an (Egalitarian) Therapist." CBE Blog/Magazine. August 5, 2020. www.cbeinternational.org/resource/article/mutuality-blog-magazine/how-find-egalitarian-therapist.

Porter, Jeanne. *Leading Lessons: Insights on Leadership from Women of the Bible*. Minneapolis: Augsburg, 2005.

RESOURCES FOR FINDING A THERAPIST

American Association for Marriage and Family Therapy. www.aamft.org/Directories/Find_a_Therapist.aspx.

American Association of Christian Counselors. www.aacc.net/resources.

American Psychological Association. www.apa.org/helpcenter.

Christian Association for Psychological Studies. https://caps.net/online-directory/.

National Board for Certified Counselors. www.nbcc.org/search/counselorfind.

Social Workers in the US. www.healthgrades.com/social-work-directory.

6

BUILDING A SUPPORT SYSTEM

One important component of achieving any goal is to surround ourselves with those who will help rather than hinder our progress—those who have our best interest at heart and want to see us succeed. In this chapter, we will consider how to build a support system to provide the guidance, role modeling, and practical help that will facilitate the process. Specifically, we will consider the importance of friends and extended family to bolster your resolve and the role of the spouse (for those who marry) in helping create a home environment conducive to success. We will also explore the value of connecting with likeminded individuals and those who can guide you into occupational opportunities.

FRIENDS AND EXTENDED FAMILY

Friends and extended family can be sources of support, offering encouragement, advice, and practical help as you work toward your goals. In fact, parental support was identified as one of the main contributors to the success of the professional women I interviewed. Some of the support came implicitly as they were raised without gendered restrictions. For others, it was more explicit. One told me her father encouraged her to keep applying for medical school after she was denied and wanted to give up. She applied again and was accepted. One reported that she would find notes left in her study area encouraging her to "reach for the stars." Another, who has a doctorate in communications, remembers her father telling her that she was capable of doctoral work if she wanted to pursue it.

In fact, most of these women identified their fathers as being especially instrumental in setting their sights toward achievement. Research suggests that a strong father-daughter relationship is related to the daughter's empowerment as well as her self-esteem and academic success.[1]

If your family and friends are not familiar with the work you plan to do, fill them in. Tell them what the major milestones will be in your education or career path—where you feel the most confident or the challenges you anticipate. Let them know that their support will be a source of encouragement for you. Share your disappointments. Celebrate with them when you succeed. They will feel a greater investment when you make them part of the journey.

Don't minimize the importance of support you will need as a man in order to be an egalitarian partner for your wife. While your commitment to equality will elicit the respect of many, you might find yourself answering for your choices more than you'd like.

Those who embrace traditional gender roles may warn you of the dangers of breaking tradition. One young man, after sharing with

---

[1]For information on the father-daughter relationship and empowerment, see Kylie M. Steinhilber et al., "Father-Daughter Relationship Dynamics and Daughters' Body Image, Eating Patterns, and Empowerment: An Exploratory Study," *Women & Health* 60, no. 10 (2020): 1083, https://doi.org/10.1080/03630242.2020.1801554. For information on the father-daughter relationship and self-esteem and academic success, see Asbah Zia, Anila Amber Malik, and Saima Masoom Ali, "Father and Daughter Relationship and Its Impact on Daughter's Self-Esteem and Academic Achievement," *Academic Journal of Interdisciplinary Studies* 4, no. 1 (2015): 311, and Shauna M. Cooper, "Associations Between Father-Daughter Relationship Quality and the Academic Engagement of African American Adolescent Girls: Self-Esteem as a Mediator?," *Journal of Black Psychology* 35, no. 4 (2009): 495, https://doi.org/10.1177/0095798409339185.

his family that he supported women following their call, was warned about the danger of diverging from the "true way to live."

Others who believe nurturing is gender-specific might question your ability. Such was the case when one of my former students in his twenties and a new father decided to be a stay-at-home dad while in graduate school. As his wife worked full-time, this arrangement served this young family well. Nevertheless, his extended family advised him that the pressure might be too much for him. So far, he hasn't found a group of other dads to plug into as he had hoped and knows of only one other man who is following the same path. However, he isn't without support as most have affirmed his decision.

FUTURE SPOUSE

Arguably, a spouse has the greatest capacity to influence our life choices and help us create a home environment conducive to achieving our goals. If you are single and consider marriage as a possibility, realize the impact a potential spouse can have on the way you live out your call. Think about the kind of partnership you aspire to have and work toward that from the beginning of any relationship you enter. Weave your call and future occupational expectations into your conversations early on. Specifically, consider the following talking points.

Egalitarian ideology. Does your partner believe in equality between women and men? What do each of you mean by *equality*? The term means different things to different people. Does he believe your call is as important as his? Or does he believe that supporting her husband's dream *is* the wife's call? Does she take her own potential seriously? Does she use direct communication so you are as clear about her calling as you are your own?

Career. How much time do each of you expect to put into your education, career preparation, and time at work? If you are not in church work, do you each still see your own and the other's work as a calling—something God-led and therefore as sacred as what happens within the church walls?

Children. How many children do you want to have, and at what points in your career do you want to have them? Who will take off of work and for how long when a child is born or adopted into the family? How do each of you feel about out-of-home childcare? How will you divide childcare responsibilities? Who will take off if a child is sick? Who will take them to doctor's visits, oversee homework, or supervise afterschool activities? Will one of you take on the role of primary caregiver? If so, what household responsibilities will the other spouse take on to help compensate for the primary caregiver's time?

Household responsibilities. Who will be responsible for which household tasks? Are you each willing to learn new skills to create an equitable balance? How will you avoid criticizing the other spouse when a task isn't done the way you would do it yourself?

Check out the recommended readings at the end of this chapter for more guidance on planning an egalitarian marriage.

SPOUSE

If you are a woman who is looking to broaden her professional opportunities, it is imperative that you communicate with your spouse throughout your journey and that you encourage him to voice any of his own concerns. Speak with him about the messages you have received and how they have affected the choices you have made. Talk with him about your call, how you feel, what you think, and any transitions you foresee. Make this an ongoing conversation so he will have the chance to catch up with where you are in the process and to emphasize the seriousness of your resolve.

Keep in mind that while this is an exciting time of change for you, the change might be unwelcome for your spouse. As discussed in chapter two, the traditional distribution of labor results in wives taking more responsibility for housework, childcare, shopping, meal preparation, and laundry. If you are currently doing these tasks, renegotiating the family workload will likely be necessary. Depending on the extent of these changes, his responsibilities might increase, which will affect how he spends his time at home and the amount of time he spends at work, in leisure, and so on.

Since the perception of a fair distribution of household responsibilities is related to couples' perceived social support,[2] it's important that you create a division of labor that each of you agree is fair. Take into account the number of hours each of you will spend in occupational pursuits when divvying up everyday household chores. Guard against assigning jobs based on who has more experience and therefore is more comfortable with any given task. As described in chapter one, a host of childhood experiences have given females a greater comfort level with most household jobs. This is one reason women end up doing a disproportionate amount of them. Remember, no one is born knowing how to make a child's lunch or sort laundry. But you can each learn new skills if it's the most effective way to balance the needs and goals each of you has set.

Keep in mind that women are more likely than men to hedge in their communication. If this is true for you, take care to be direct. Have reasonable expectations. Don't apologize for your desire to fulfill your call; don't expect him to apologize for his. State your expectations clearly. Listen to his. Be willing to negotiate, but don't assume your husband can't do the same.

Consider the agreements you made in the past, either explicitly or implicitly. You might have agreed to take full responsibility for the

[2]Marieke Van Willigen and Patricia Drentea, "Benefits of Equitable Relationships: The Impact of Sense of Fairness, Household Division of Labor, and Decision Making Power on Perceived Social Support," *Sex Roles* 44, no. 9/10 (2001): 571.

children each weekday evening. Maybe it seemed right when you offered to do all meal prep and the cleanup afterwards. But if the arrangement doesn't work for you now, renegotiation is reasonable. Marriages are living covenants that ideally evolve as the individuals in them grow.

One of my friends shared with me how the household distribution of labor shifted when his wife made the decision to go back to school after unexpectedly losing her job. He gave up a few hobbies to devote more time to meal preparation and housework. But, as he reminded me, she had done the same when he had made a career change a few years before. "Giving her room to live her dream was easy. We are partners, and that is just what we do. She stood by me as I left a much higher-paying job to live my dream." The result? They are now *both* living their dreams. With pride, he told me, "She is a leader and one of the strongest people I know."

If you are a man whose wife is moving toward broader opportunities, keep the following in mind: You have been shaped by a culture that too often sees your needs and goals as the driving force behind family plans. These influences have implicitly influenced your self-perceptions and the expectations you have for a spouse. Be sensitive to your own sense of entitlement. It is never my goal to shame men for having bought into a patriarchal mindset; we all have—that's the point. Men are as much victims of socialization as are women. But sometimes a woman's call for equality can feel like oppression to those who enjoy privilege. And while you should not be held responsible for centuries of male privilege, do be sensitive to the ways you have benefited from it and the power you have to enact change within your own sphere of influence.

What can you do? Listen to your spouse. Ask yourself if what she requests of you would seem reasonable if they were *your* requests of *her*. If so, cooperate with her to achieve a balance that will provide equal opportunities for the two of you. If not, work with her to create a more equitable arrangement.

Specific guidelines for navigating change within marriage are beyond the scope of this book. However, the information here can provide the starting point for effective communication between you and your spouse.

CONNECT WITH LIKEMINDED PEOPLE

Others have taken the same journey you now face. Connecting with those people can provide you a rich source of guidance and encouragement. They can let you know the terrain to expect, where the roadblocks are, the detours that are quickest, and where to find rest stops when the road seems impossibly long.

Organizations. Plugging into organizations that promote equal opportunities for women can help you reach your goals while encouraging the same in others. As society has become increasingly aware of the personal and systemic obstacles women face, organizations to help counter those obstacles are more available than ever before. Find a group within your field and explore the resources they offer. Most professional organizations host conferences, publish journals, and provide networking opportunities that can be an ongoing source of guidance along your career path.[3] Other organizations focus on personal and/or professional issues pertinent to girls

[3]For information on organizations for women in STEM fields, see the websites for the Association for Women in Science at www.awis.org, Women in Technology International at https://witi.com/, Society for Women Engineers at https://swe.org, the Association for Women in Mathematics at https://awm-math.org. For information on the American Medical Women's Association, see www.amwa-doc.org; International Federation of Business and Professional Women, see www.bpw-international.org; Financial Women's Association, see www.fwa.org; the American Association of University Women, see www.aauw.org; National Association of Women in Construction, see www.nawic.org/nawic/default.asp; Women's Caucus for Art, see https://nationalwca.org; Women in Film and Television International, see www.wifti.net; the Institute for Biblical Research—IBR Women, see https://ibr-bbr.org/about/ibr-women; and the International Association of Women Ministers, see http://womenministers.org/site/welcome.

and women in general[4] and to issues surrounding the Christian faith in particular;[5] these provide resources useful across a variety of occupations and areas of personal interest.

While these organizations are primarily composed of women, they usually welcome the participation of men who take seriously the challenges women face. If you are a man who wants to build a more equitable world for women, consider donating your time to one or more of these organizations. Not only will you grow in your own awareness, but you will be contributing to the change you wish to see for your mothers, sisters, and daughters.

One organization, Christians for Biblical Equality (CBE), has specifically benefited me both personally and professionally.[6] CBE provides guidance through articles written by women and men of all ages from around the world who have started their lives in restrictive mindsets regarding gender and moved into truth and the freedom it brings. Their conferences have encouraged me and countless others in making the journey and introduced me to people and ideas I never would have known otherwise. In addition, local chapters provide a way to find other likeminded people in one's geographic area and ways to plug into local events that provide education and service opportunities.

CBE's work is marked with grace as they educate the world about the scriptural basis for equality between women and men. They model patience and kindness with those who struggle to understand the egalitarian position; they have helped me do the same.

When I first began teaching gender studies at the small, Baptist university where I am on faculty, I was convinced of the egalitarian

---

[4]For information on InterVarsity Women in the Academy and Professions, see https://thewell.intervarsity.org; the International Association of Women, see https://careers.iawomen.com; the National Organization for Women, see https://now.org; Girls Inc., see https://girlsinc.org/about-us; and the YWCA, see www.ywca.org.

[5]Christians for Biblical Equality, Website Homepage, www.cbeinternational.org.

[6]Christians for Biblical Equality, Website Homepage, www.cbeinternational.org.

philosophy but struggled with how to present it. The material was new to most of my students, and they understandably needed time to mull over and absorb the content. Yet I felt frustrated with their hesitancy to accept the material I presented and what I saw as my inability to make them see what I saw so clearly.

It was during this time that I found CBE and began to see the value of unapologetic conviction tempered with nonjudgmental grace. I learned a great deal from their approach, and I became a better teacher for it. Today I am much more understanding of the process of change and the need to let people grow at their own pace.

I'm grateful for discovering CBE during that point in my life. I encourage you to find an organization or two that can provide support for your own journey and a way to contribute to a more equitable world.

Social media. Social media is another tool through which you can connect with likeminded people. One such group is the Biblical Christian Egalitarians (BCE) group on Facebook. Their stated mission is to help readers "Believe, connect, and engage with egalitarians who value equality in Christ, support women's ordination, and share leadership in marriage."[7] I appreciate the posts I read there from people who are at different points in their understanding of gender and faith. Some are just starting their journey. They are asking the same questions I asked several decades ago when I had a hunch that there was another way to look at things. Some of them are farther along than I am, and model for me ways to handle interactions with those whose opinions differ from my own. While there is a great deal of religious and political diversity among its followers, they work to keep the focus on the commonalities we share as we work toward equality at home and within our churches.

---

[7]Biblical Christian Egalitarians, Facebook, www.facebook.com/groups/BiblicalChristianEgalitarians.

In addition, many of the organizations mentioned in the last section provide opportunities for networking and discussion through social media.

Less formal are the connections we make through our personal social media presence. It doesn't take long for our "friends" and "followers" to identify what we are passionate about. To the extent that you can be open about your beliefs, you will likely find a host of likeminded people among those you already know.

Church. The church holds some of the greatest potential for supporting equality between men and women. Unfortunately, the church also presents some of the greatest obstacles to the same. One professional woman I interviewed reported that she grew up in a non-Christian home where she was told she could be anything she wanted. It wasn't until after she began attending church that she was told otherwise. During her first year of college, she shared her decision to become a pastor with the church she had been attending and was told that women did not become pastors. To his credit, her then pastor acknowledged that it wasn't fair. "But it's just the way it is," he said. She could be a missionary, he told her, and do all the things a pastor does. She just couldn't pastor. Others in her congregation suggested she go to a Bible college, get a husband, and raise their children. She tried for a while to conform to their expectations, but they didn't fit with the person she knew herself to be. Thankfully, she concluded that they were mistaken and eventually followed her call into the pastorate.

Likewise, a professional woman spoke to me of her disappointment that the secular culture often leads the way in freeing women. She told me, "I wish the church would lead the way instead." Her work as a business consultant as well as her leadership within her own church are moving both in the right direction.

One former student reported to me that he doesn't openly support women in ministry for fear of his church's reaction. When he broached the subject, he was accused of being "liberal" and told, "remember how you were raised." He tells me that their fear of women leaders extends beyond the church as they also object to women leading in government. He isn't their pastor; he isn't on their payroll. Yet he fears their reaction should he state his views with confidence.

If your church is not egalitarian, you might not find much support for your journey, whether you are a woman or a man. However, it will be especially difficult for the woman who aspires to leadership. One woman I interviewed lost her job due to layoffs at the university where she was on faculty. While her husband was also employed, hers was their primary source of income. Their church is not egalitarian and most of her church friends were not employed outside the home. She told me they didn't seem to understand the gravity of her situation. They were sympathetic but seemed to think of her income as supplemental. She wasn't concerned about cutting back on luxuries; she told me, "I was afraid we would lose our house."

While you might very well find individuals there who understand your occupational goals, there might not be enough of them to give you the support you need. If that is the case, you might need to consider whether this church is the best place to worship and grow.

I don't say this lightly. No denomination or congregation is perfect. We can disagree about a multitude of issues and still find a spiritual home among those who differ. I also understand the ties that bind us to our places of worship. Going to church with extended family and lifelong friends, the history we share with a congregation, and fears around uprooting our children from the familiar—all these factors and more can make changing churches difficult. When I have been in similar situations, I have sometimes opted to stay. Other times, I have opted to leave. It's a difficult call. But I hope your need for support will weigh in as an important factor in determining where to attend and serve.

If your church is egalitarian in its philosophy, you will likely find support for your call regardless of your sex. However, you might still find yourself held back by the same implicit messages that we have covered in this book. Those committed to equality in the church still find themselves pulled back into traditional ways of navigating home and church administration. The same media sources, home environments, and education system that shaped you, shaped the people you worship with on Sunday morning. Regardless of their support, they might still unintentionally place obstacles in your path.

For this reason, I encourage you to speak with your pastor, other church leaders, and congregants about what you are learning. Let them know of the implicit messages that have shaped you. It will give them a glimpse into your reality and shed light onto any blind spots they might have.

SEEK OUT A PROFESSIONAL GUIDE

While support from family and friends, a spouse, your church, and other organizations is important, as a woman you will also need someone to guide you into the occupation or ministry to which you aspire. Kadi Cole, author of *Developing Female Leaders*, distinguishes between mentors, sponsors, and coaches.[8] A *mentor*, she explains, serves as a role model and adviser, offering constructive feedback as we try out new skills. Mentorship often transpires between meetings, over coffee or at lunch, where the established professional lets the new hire in on the unwritten rules that govern the workplace. Similarly, a *sponsor* opens "organizational doors, advocates for opportunities, connects [us] with influential leaders."[9] Cole suggests that for a woman in a male-dominated occupation, having a man to mentor and sponsor her will give her greater

[8]Kadi Cole, *Developing Female Leaders* (Nashville, TN: Thomas Nelson, 2019), 80-89.
[9]Cole, *Developing Female Leaders*, 84.

insight into the inner workings of the organization and entry into its leadership.[10]

One pastor described the obstacles she faced in finding her first pastorate. While her denomination readily ordained women, she had not been raised in church so was uninformed regarding how to put her name in for pastor positions. She went to seminary but did not have a mentor to prepare her for life after graduation nor a sponsor to usher her into the network of denominational life. It was years before she learned the process and was called by a church to be their pastor. A male mentor or sponsor could have accelerated the process.

However, even the most effective male mentor or sponsor will not know the unique challenges and expectations you will experience as a woman. For instance, your male mentor likely did not become an organizational leader while carrying the lion's share of his family's childcare and household responsibilities. For guidance here, Cole states, we will benefit most from a woman who has successfully met these challenges herself to *coach* us.[11]

Many find a mentor, sponsor, or coach while in school. College and graduate school faculty often fill these roles as their students transition from academia to the workforce. Get to know your professors. Share your story and listen to theirs.

Likewise, many older colleagues will fill this role for young professionals who are eager to learn. Find a seasoned professional within your church or organization, someone who embodies the personal and professional characteristics you want to hone. Let them know you value their insight and would appreciate their guidance.

Professional organizations also offer opportunities to learn from those who have been in the profession for decades and who are eager

[10]Cole, *Developing Female Leaders*, 80-85.
[11]Cole, *Developing Female Leaders*, 85-89.

to share their knowledge about the field. Find an organization with goals that are in line with your own and attend its meetings regularly. Take advantage of any services they provide to help you connect with others of similar interests but greater experience.

Your journey will be easier with a strong support system. Enlisting the support of your friends and family, building a home environment conducive to your call, walking alongside other likeminded people, and building professional connections are each important in fulfilling your call to leadership and supporting the same in your spouse.

RECOMMENDED READING

Howell, Susan, and Dwayne Howell. "Our Dual-Career Family: Benefits and Challenges." CBE. Spring 2009. www.cbeinternational.org/resource/article/our-dual-career-family.

Morgante, Camden. "Egalitarian from the Start: 4 Practical Tips for New Parents." CBE Blog/Magazine. August 13, 2019. www.cbeinternational.org/resource/article/mutuality-blog-magazine/egalitarian-start-4-practical-tips-new-parents.

Morgante, Camden. "Egalitarian from the Start: Practical Tips for Engagements and Weddings." CBE Blog/Magazine. July 16, 2019. www.cbeinternational.org/resource/article/mutuality-blog-magazine/egalitarian-start-practical-tips-engagements-and-weddings.

Quient, Nicholas Rudolph. "How I Submit to My Wife: Why a Feminist with a Hairy Chest Chose to Take His Beloved's Last Name." CBE. December 4, 2015. www.cbeinternational.org/resource/article/mutuality-blog-magazine/how-i-submit-my-wife-why-feminist-hairy-chest-chose-take.

Van Leeuwen, Mary Stewart. *Gender and Grace: Love, Work and Parenting in a Changing World.* Downers Grove, IL: InterVarsity Press, 1990.

7

PAYING IT FORWARD

One way to solidify the learning of new information is to put it into practice. For this reason, we will now explore ways to use what you have learned to make a difference in the lives of others. First, we will explore actions you can implement at the microlevel—within your interpersonal relationships—to send constructive messages about gender and achievement to those closest to you. Second, we will consider measures you can pursue at the macrolevel—within the institutions of your community—to influence the systemic processes that shape the collective mindset of our culture. Through your interpersonal interactions and extending your influence into your local schools, your church, the workplace, and places where you do business, your actions will have far-reaching effects for the girls of today and the women of tomorrow.

MICROLEVEL ACTIONS

At the microlevel, you have the capacity to influence many on a day-to-day basis. Whether raising children, sharing a holiday with extended family and friends, or chatting with a coworker over lunch, you can affect others' gendered perceptions by creating a culture of empowerment and promptly correcting any misperceptions that arise.

Create a culture of empowerment. If you plan to have children, raising them in a culture of empowerment will be easier if that culture is in place before your child is born. For this reason, it is essential that you and the child's other parent are in agreement on the importance of gender equality and how you plan to foster it.

If you are a man planning fatherhood, consider taking paternity leave. Many employers now offer male employees the opportunity to be home with their newborns. Avoid thinking of this as a chance to "help out" at home; instead, think of it as a time for adapting to your new role and developing a bond with your son or daughter. One educator said her husband not only took paternity leave but also extended his stay at home for an additional month after she returned to her full-time job. Her husband is now a competent and confident parent to their two-year-old daughter. Another told me that her husband would be insulted if she corrected how he fed, diapered, or otherwise cared for their new son. "He knows as much about him as I do," she told me with pride. And your actions today can benefit your children for years to come, in that "fathers with more egalitarian gender-role beliefs had daughters and sons who were equally likely to imagine balancing work and family in the future."[1]

Likewise, if you are a new mother, avoid criticizing the other parent's style of caregiving. It's more important that the child have two loving, involved parents than to have everything done your way. In addition, consistent criticism sends an implicit message that you are the parent in charge, the one who is ultimately responsible for the child's care. This will undermine the culture you hope to create.

Select toys that teach the importance of caring for a home and children along with those that take them outside the home into

---

[1] Alyssa Croft et al., "The Second Shift Reflected in the Second Generation: Do Parents' Gender Roles at Home Predict Children's Aspirations?," *Psychological Science* 25, no. 7 (2014): 1424, https://doi.org/10.1177/0956797614533968.

physical activity, scientific exploration, and an understanding of the world. Expose them to a variety of activities to see what they gravitate toward. It might be your only chance to find out what they want before others tell them what they *should* want.

While you will have less influence over the children of others, you can still give them gifts that encourage a balance of interests. Your grandchildren, nieces and nephews, and children of friends will benefit from your gifting according to their interests rather than assuming she gets the doll, and he gets the video game. Consider gender-neutral toys, and given the opportunity, break the stereotypes altogether. When our son was born a friend bought our three-year-old daughter a doctor's kit so she could "help" take care of him. We appreciated this nontraditional gift and the message it sent.

As any child in your life matures, continue to encourage a variety of interests, paying particular attention to their natural talents and abilities. Ask about her science experiment. If others downplay her inclination toward math, cheer her on. And take care to affirm his nontraditional pursuits as evidence of strength, not weakness. When he cradles a doll, see his potential for being a sensitive father. If he forgoes team sports but loves cooking, find a recipe you can make together.

Likewise, be intentional about the chores you assign, including a mix of the traditionally feminine and masculine for your daughters and your sons. Teach your sons that laundry and childcare are as much their responsibility as anyone else's. This will develop their skill and confidence in these tasks and prevent their holding unreasonable expectations for a future partner.

Make a variety of books available, taking care to find those with females whose achievements and contributions are showcased. While this will foster self-esteem in your daughter or niece, your son or nephew will also learn that women are as capable as males of accomplishing things that matter. Provide an assortment of movies and television programs and encourage a balance in their viewing.

Watch your language. Minimize androcentric words and phrases. Take care to compliment girls more on their talent than on their looks. One professional woman in academia told me that she and her husband are intentional when labeling their young daughter's behavior. Rather than *bossy*, she has *strong leadership skills*. She isn't *strong-willed*; she *knows what she wants*. This mother had been shamed as a child for some of her own personality characteristics and didn't want the same for her daughter.

These modifications will send positive messages to the adults in your life as well. Your adjustment of business*man* to business*person* could be the reframe your friend needs as she contemplates a career change. When your nephew becomes a nurse, referring to him as such, rather than classifying him as a *male* nurse, will be welcomed. Even if your friend is a mother, don't reference her children in every conversation. Ask about her work and other interests. She is more than someone's mother, as rewarding as that can be. Words communicate our perceptions and influence the perceptions others acquire. Use them wisely.

Since the world will likely encourage the girls in your life to minimize their occupational potential, take care that she hears a different message from you. Discuss careers early and often. Help her identify a variety of occupations that would make good use of her gifts and abilities. If you hear about a woman with talents similar to hers, let your granddaughter know how they are using that talent in a career. This is especially important when that career is unique, not something she is likely to know about already. Have you read an interesting article about a woman who achieved in a nontraditional area? The woman in your Sunday school class who is going back to school might enjoy reading it.

Guard against asking that girl at church how many children she wants when she grows up. Or at least don't ask her any more frequently than you ask her brother. Likewise, take care not to equate having a career with success for the boys in your Sunday school class while downplaying its importance for the girls.

Help her feel competent in activities the world labels as masculine. One way of doing so is through the kind of help you provide with homework. Simply telling the child what to do communicates a lack of confidence in her abilities. For instance, your daughter doesn't have a topic for her speech, so you give her one. She doesn't understand how to complete a science project, so you read through the instructions and tell her how to do it.

In contrast, autonomy-granting assistance nudges the child in the right direction without taking control. Instead of giving her a speech topic, ask her what interests she has that her classmates would enjoying hearing about. Instead of explaining the science project instructions, help her talk through the part she doesn't understand so she can decide how to proceed. This method would seem to affirm the child's competence. Indeed, mothers' autonomy-granting has been identified as part of a dynamic interplay associated with child task persistence in early-elementary-school-aged children.[2] In subjects that are traditionally seen as masculine and for which confidence is important,[3] autonomy-granting could be particularly helpful for girls.

---

[2]Jaana Viljaranta et al., "Maternal Homework Assistance and Children's Task-Persistent Behavior in Elementary School," *Learning and Instruction* 56 (2018): 60, https://doi.org/10.1016/j.learninstruc.2018.04.005.

[3]For information on the importance of confidence in subjects traditionally considered masculine, see Gail Crombie et al., "Predictors of Young Adolescents' Math Grades and Course Enrollment Intentions: Gender Similarities and Differences," *Sex Roles* 52, no. 5/6 (2005): 351, https://doi.org/10.1007/s11199-005-2678-1; Wei-Cheng Mau, "Factors That Influence Persistence in Science and Engineering Career Aspirations," *The Career Development Quarterly* 51 (March 2003): 234; and Carol A. Heaverlo, Robyn Cooper, and Frankie Santos Lannan, "STEM Development: Predictors for 6th-12th Grade Girls' Interest and Confidence in Science and Math," *Journal of Women and Minorities in Science and Engineering* 19, no. 2 (2013): 121-42.

While adult friends might not need homework help, they probably do seek your advice from time to time. Giving advice, particularly in areas where you have specialized knowledge, can be helpful. But offering autonomy-granting assistance is more appropriate if they simply need someone to help them process their options.

Teach your children the importance of who they partner with as adults. This will have special importance for girls as they are more likely to one day have a spouse who expects their own career to come first. Help the girls in your life see the value of selecting partners who appreciate their abilities and respect their responsibility to follow God's call.

While following these suggestions will send an abundance of implicit messages, why not go a step further and make the messages explicit? Tell your children why you have them alternate dinner cleanup. Voice your rationale for giving both trucks and dolls for Christmas. Explain why you are careful not to provide too much homework help. In letting them in on your reasoning, you provide a template they can use when making decisions on their own.

One day a student approached me after my lecture on gender and moral reasoning to tell me she had just realized something: She had been holding back from planning her own career because she didn't want to inconvenience her new husband. That lecture had been the first time she received an explicit message that ran counter to the many implicit messages she had received over the years. Had I not made it explicit, she might not have realized it until much later, past the time when opportunities would be the easiest to pursue. I don't know what option she eventually chose, but I do know that she made her choice after hearing explicitly that gender affects choices and how to mediate those effects.

And with all your relationships, let your life reflect the values you hold. Model the importance of following God's call, even when it breaks the norms others have set. Share your own experiences, where you have struggled, the barriers you faced, and how you broke through them. Much of what we learn comes through watching what others do. Take that seriously.

Correct misperceptions. As children get older, they increasingly receive messages from multiple sources. Therefore, it is important to correct any misinformation they seem to be picking up. When our three-year-old son chattered about the toys in the church nursery, he referred to "the girls area." When I asked what that meant, he described the kitchen set, dishes, and dolls they had played with the week before. I gently reminded him that his father and I both prepared meals and cared for him and his sister; that these tasks were done by all people, not just girls and women. The entire conversation took no more than a couple of minutes but reminded me to listen as he talked about his world and what he was learning about that world from people outside our household.

Likewise, notice what your friend says about herself, both directly and indirectly. Is she overly self-critical? Remind her of her strengths. Is she tempted to quit trying? Encourage her to continue working for her dreams. If she says things that run counter to the evidence, gently challenge her. Share one of the recommended readings in this book. Invite her to read a book with you and discuss its application. You can also be direct; let her know if you think she is selling herself short. Let the nature of your relationship and the level of closeness you share determine what to say and to what degree.

Of course, some of the faulty messages out there come directly from us, no matter how much we try to empower others. Just because we intend to send messages of equality, does not mean we are always successful. Telling my children that women are courageous probably fell on deaf ears when I would back away, present my disgusted look, and ask my husband to kill any spider that crept into my field of vision. When I realized I was sending a louder message with my actions than my words, I began killing those spiders myself. (By the way, this is an example of *behaving as if* that I described in chapter five and did, indeed, result in my fear diminishing considerably.)

Notice how children speak about leisure activities, household tasks, or subjects in school. When your niece says she hates math, ask her about it. If your grandson rolls his eyes when a teenage girl preaches on youth Sunday, ask him about it. Provide evidence to the contrary if they have received faulty information and offer them an alternate perspective.

Notice if they seem to lose interest in school subjects or hobbies they once enjoyed. While identity development often requires a focus on some interests over others, pay attention to whether that focus is biased by gendered expectations. Remember the tendency during middle school for girls to minimize their own success? Notice when her grades go down or she pulls away from a sport she had always loved. Ask about it. Remind her that women have diverse interests that do not always fit into gender stereotypes. So do men.

As they begin thinking about future occupations, help expand the possibilities they consider. If your daughter has made excellent grades in science but tells you she cannot be a doctor, ask her about it. If your son is great with children but will not even consider teaching elementary school, ask him about it. While a person's career choice should be their own, it is appropriate to clarify whether she is second-guessing her abilities and if he is diminishing the value of an occupation because it is usually done by women.

If you sense that your daughter is not using her voice, encourage her to speak up. Find out what she imagines might happen if she were to speak her opinion with confidence. Does she believe her opinions aren't important? Or that they will make her unpopular with her peers? Does she doubt she can make a difference? Has someone told her that she is bossy?

One program utilized role play to help elementary-school-aged girls develop alternative, assertive responses to situations they had experienced in school.[4] These girls wanted to avoid bragging, so role playing was to help them "feel good about achieving while maintaining the friendship and support they value[d]."[5] Find out what is holding your daughter back and role play with her ways to speak up until she feels comfortable doing so.

By sending messages that empower and correcting misperceptions as they arise you can provide a multitude of messages that will empower the children and adults in your life.

MACROLEVEL ACTIONS

I challenge you, however, to not stop there. Change needs to happen within the institutions that have helped create a culture that downplays the abilities of women. Harnessing the power of these systems can make our personal efforts more effective in bringing about lasting change. In this section, we will explore ways to make a difference in your schools, your church, the workplace, and within the businesses that promote a limited mindset for girls and women.

Schools in your community. Become informed regarding the policies and practices within your local schools. One way to do so is to volunteer. Whether you volunteer within the classroom on a regular basis or must limit yourself to chaperoning a field trip, you will gain insight about the messages your child receives on a day-to-day basis. For instance, does the teacher call on one sex more often than the other? Does he use language that includes girls and women? Do field trips take your child to places that welcome the

---

[4]Lee Anne Bell, "In Danger of Winning: Consciousness Raising Strategies for Empowering Girls in the United States," *Women's Studies International Forum* 19, no. 4 (1996): 420-21.
[5]Bell, "In Danger of Winning," 421-22.

employment of both men and women? What about guest speakers? Do they showcase the accomplishments of men and women from a variety of occupations?

What about the nonacademic interactions within the classroom? Are boys asked to rearrange chairs while girls are asked to decorate the bulletin board? Are boys pitted against the girls in classroom or school-wide contests, or are they encouraged to work together as peers?

Even if you cannot spend time in the classroom, notice the textbooks your child brings home. Are they all written by men? Do history texts include peripheral sections on the contributions of women, or are they woven throughout, normalizing the value of their accomplishments?

When you find problems that need to be addressed, remember these are often unintentional and can be modified easily by raising awareness. Remember that teachers and school officials are also recipients of a barrage of implicit messages. But given that some gender stereotypes emerge as early as third grade, early intervention is crucial.[6]

The website for the Let Toys Be Toys campaign provides suggestions for raising awareness when you notice inequity in the classroom and is included in the recommended reading at the end of this chapter. Among their suggestions are speaking with your child's teacher about your concerns, offering an alternative to the practice you find harmful, and presenting research evidence to counter any misconceptions they have.[7] Their website also includes a template to help present your concerns in clear, assertive

[6]Jennifer Herbert and Deborah Stipek, "The Emergence of Gender Differences in Children's Perceptions of Their Academic Competence," *Applied Developmental Psychology* 26 (2005): 290, https://doi.org/10.1016/j.appdev.2005.02.007.

[7]"Raising a Concern with Your Child's School," Let Toys Be Toys, www.lettoysbetoys.org.uk/resources/parents-raising-an-issue-with-your-childs-school.

language and includes links to research relevant to a variety of gender issues.

And when you notice the school's efforts to combat gender inequity, be generous in your appreciation. Let the teacher and school administration know that their efforts have not gone unnoticed.

Advocate for career education. Reaching girls early in the education process is cited by multiple researchers as an important component to equalizing opportunities for women.[8] Likewise, providing role models for girls who want to balance career and family is suggested for increasing the number of women in male-dominated fields and to address the tendency for women to choose careers that underutilize their abilities.[9]

One way to do this is through career education throughout all levels of the education process. If the schools in your community have career days, volunteer to assist. If they do not, offer to help establish one as a regular part of the academic year. Recruit a diverse sample of individuals, male and female, to participate. Professionals from your community can showcase what they do, the subjects they studied, and the education required for their occupation. In addition, having professional women discuss obstacles they have overcome would be especially helpful for older girls who realize they are disadvantaged and lack role models to help them navigate the

[8]Gillian Marks and Diane M. Houston, "The Determinants of Young Women's Intentions About Education, Career Development and Family Life," *Journal of Education and Work* 15, no. 3 (2002): 321, https://doi.org/10.1080/1363908022000012085, and Melanie C. Steffens et al., "On the Leaky Math Pipeline: Comparing Implicit Math-Gender Stereotypes and Math Withdrawal in Female and Male Children and Adolescents," *Journal of Educational Psychology* 102, no. 4 (2010): 960-61, https://doi.org/10.1037/a0019920.

[9]For information on increasing the number of women in male-dominated fields, see Pamela M. Frome et al., "Why Don't They Want a Male-Dominated Job? An Investigation of Young Women Who Changed Their Occupational Aspirations," *Educational Research and Evaluation* 12, no. 4 (2006): 369, https://doi.org/10.1080/13803610600765786. For information on addressing the tendency to underutilize one's abilities, see Karen M. O'Brien et al., "Attachment, Separation, and Women's Vocational Development: A Longitudinal Analysis," *Journal of Counseling Psychology* 47, no. 3 (2000): 312, https://doi.org/10.1037//0022-0167.47.3.301.

challenges. Introduce the girls in your community to women who have succeeded in a broad range of occupations, including those that are male dominated. As Pamela M. Frome and colleagues suggest, "Find the exceptions to the 'rule' and publicize them widely."[10]

If you have a daughter or granddaughter, ask her to partner with you in this endeavor. Her contribution to making a difference within her own school will help her develop a sense of agency in prompting systemic changes. In her article on consciousness-raising strategies, Lee Anne Bell emphasizes the importance of collective action as she utilized elementary school girls to help plan and implement their school's career day.[11] She says that these girls learned that "problems they see are not given and immutable but rather obstacles that can be challenged and changed."[12]

Your church. You can also have an impact within your church. Take note of the Scripture translation used by your pastor and those who lead children and youth. If they are not already doing so, suggest they consider moving to a translation that is gender accurate. Articles that explain some of the issues pertinent to the language of Scripture are listed in the recommended reading at the end of this chapter. Share one of them to begin the conversation. Similarly, if the music selection tends toward androcentric language, you might approach the music minister about songs that are more inclusive of women's gifts and calling.

Does your pastor make jokes that demean or marginalize women? While usually spoken without malice, such comments are harmful as they depict women and girls as comical, concerned with petty matters, or less deserving of respect. Some parishioners are hesitant to approach a religious leader to complain about something that was

---

[10]Frome et al., "Why Don't They Want," 369.
[11]Bell, "In Danger of Winning," 426.
[12]Bell, "In Danger of Winning," 427.

intended as harmless banter. I have received an eye roll or two for making "too big of a deal out of a joke." But I challenge you: the next time you hear a derogatory remark made from the pulpit about women—even in jest—ask yourself this: How would it sound if the object of the comment had been a person of another race? Would it have been offensive? If so, then it was inappropriate when levied against women. You are not being overly sensitive. You have a right to bring it to that person's attention. A good leader should be able to hear constructive criticism and make changes when warranted.

You could also teach a class on gender equality at your church using this book or any of the resources at the end of these chapters. Select the topic based on what will be best received. A congregation might not be ready for a discussion on women pastors but might consider a marriage workshop on communicating needs more effectively. Your church might not be ready to ordain women as deacons, but a class on how each of us—male and female—can discern God's call would be accepted. While these are small steps, they are relevant to empowering women and could still move your congregation in the right direction.

Depending on the resources within your church or larger community, make training events such as these a regular practice. Enlist a variety of women and men from various fields of study to share their expertise. Hearing the same message from multiple perspectives—theology, psychology, sociology—will emphasize the accuracy and importance of the message. Are resources limited? Host a book club in your home in which you lead discussions on books relevant for women's growth. These groups need not be large to empower a woman who needs the message.

You could offer to serve on a church committee or special project to encourage a broader perspective on gender. Over the past several decades, I have worked to broaden the gendered perspective of each church I have attended. I have taught classes where I had the say in which topics I covered and the material I used. Other times, my participation merely kept women from being dismissed as equal partners in the work of the church. I have served on committees where I reminded them of the woman's perspective. I have spoken up as a choir member when the language for a special selection excluded the contributions women have made. I have spoken my opinion in more Bible studies than I can count when narrow interpretations of Scripture have minimized the usefulness of women to God's work. At times, my contributions were small, but I was always persistent.

However, your congregation might be open to bolder initiatives. Would they consider a woman when searching for a new pastor? Would they consider having a woman speak to the congregation for a special service within her area of expertise? In addition to expanding the experience of the church body, this will provide a valuable role model for the girls and women within your congregation.

Several women I interviewed spoke of not having a female role model when preparing for ministry. One shared that she had never actually heard a woman preach. She wondered if women even preached the same as men. Did they use the same style or tone of voice? When she later heard a woman speak, she was taken with how natural she sounded. She knew then that she could simply be herself. The boys in your congregation who aspire to the ministry of preaching will have a lifetime of male preachers with a variety of styles to guide in the development of their own. The way to stand, the tone of voice, the physical mannerisms to avoid or hone. For girls to envision themselves in this role, they too will benefit from role models.

Of course, what you do and how you do it depends on your church's position on equality between men and women. If your church is egalitarian, its leadership will likely welcome your efforts. However, they will still have blind spots, as do we all, and might still benefit from increased awareness of implicit socialization.

If your church is complementarian, try to find common ground from which you can build a relationship of mutual respect with its leaders and members. For instance, some congregations support women preaching as long as they don't pastor. Some allow women to pastor as long as a man holds the title of *senior pastor*. As an egalitarian, I still see this as unnecessarily limiting of women, but the commitment we share to broadening women's opportunities allows us a space from which we can work together.

Over the years, I have been asked to teach classes by those who held a more traditional perspective on relationships. Some who see men as the rightful leaders in marriage have referred couples to me for counseling. I would like to believe that although we disagree on some things, we agree on enough to keep the conversation going.

For this reason, I suggest you begin by speaking to your pastor or church leadership about what you are learning. Ask if they are open to working to broaden the church's thinking about women's roles. Gauge whether they are eager for your involvement, willing to consider your ideas, or closed to any discussion.

If your efforts are not welcomed and discussion is impossible, you might consider whether this is the best place for you to serve. A church that does not validate your call will not give you space to exercise your gifts. Nor will it allow you to formally promote the same in others. And if you have children, consider the messages they will hear on a regular basis within that church. Even in the best of congregations, you might need to correct misconceptions your children have picked up there. However, going to a church where your children are exposed to a constant stream of inaccurate information that you cannot undo is unadvisable.

When our children were young, we would occasionally hear sermons that ran counter to what we were teaching them. The ride home on those Sundays typically found my husband and me addressing with our children what had been said and our beliefs on the topic. Thankfully, those occasions were seldom enough that we did not feel the need to find another church home. Had it happened on a more regular basis, maybe we would have.

If you choose to stay, however, let your presence and consistent reminders call them to a higher place.

Your workplace. It is as important to pay attention to practices within the workplace as it is within your schools and your church. Are both men and women well represented within management? If not, ask questions. If your place of business has made explicit efforts at recruiting women for leadership, look to the implicit factors that might be undermining even their genuine efforts at balance.

How do those who successfully climb the corporate ladder know how to get ahead? Is there a mentoring program with equal access for all? Or do men learn best practices for promotion over a golf game or at lunch with other male VIPs? Is there a gender discrepancy in pay? If so, are female applicants made aware that negotiation is an expected component of the hiring process? Do training opportunities include women? Or do they communicate that women are the anomaly and, as such, not worthy of the company's investment of resources? A recent literature review revealed that gender equity practices facilitate women moving into leadership positions, and formal leadership training programs for women help in "raising opportunities for females to be accepted as effective leaders."[13]

[13]Tamer Koburtay, Jawad Syed, and Radi Haloub, "Congruity Between the Female Gender Role and the Leader Role: A Literature Review," *European Business Review* 31, no. 6 (2019): 842-43, https://doi.org/10.1108/EBR-05-2018-0095.

Jill Richardson addresses the marginalization that women experience at conferences, seminars, and retreats.[14] While specifically addressing women in church leadership, many of her suggestions for action apply equally well to any place of employment. She suggests that women ask questions, persistently, as a first step to changing current patterns. Some of the questions she lists address using material in which female writers are represented, using material that uses gender inclusive language, and having women represented among keynote speakers.

Does your business encourage a healthy balance between work and family for male and female employees? Employer expectations were created within a culture dictating that full-time employees would be men who had wives at home handling child and house care. Unfortunately, the workplace has not adapted to the move many families have made away from this model. Business leader Eeva Sallinen Simard states, "It is no wonder so many women feel unsatisfied with the workplace: it was originally designed to keep them at home."[15]

Based on your position and the status you hold within your company, decide what is within your power to accomplish. Could you initiate a formal mentoring program that would help female colleagues learn best practices for advancement? Is there a woman you could sponsor for a leadership position who would otherwise be overlooked? Might you lobby for both paternity and maternity leave to communicate that work goals and home care are compatible?

If you have the respect of your colleagues, speak up for those who are dismissed. Is a female colleague interrupted in meetings? If so,

---

[14]Jill Richardson, "The Subtle Hazing of Women in Ministry," Christians for Biblical Equality, November 6, 2019, www.cbeinternational.org/resource/article/mutuality-blog-magazine/subtle-hazing-women-ministry.

[15]Eeva Sallinen Simard, "Women at Work: 3 Things I Wish I Knew When I Graduated College," *Mutuality*, Fall 2019, 13.

direct attention back to her. Does a male coworker reiterate ideas that originated with a female office mate and then receive credit for it? If so, remind him where he first heard the idea. One seminary professor told me that when she first began speaking up at faculty meetings, others would ignore, laugh at, or disagree with her. "They communicated that women didn't have the right to be there, and when we were there—in the man's space—we didn't deserve respect." If you have a voice, use it for those who do not.

If you are not in a position to make big changes, select a need you see as most pressing and begin a conversation with others who are able to do something. Do you have a good relationship with a manager? Make an appointment to discuss what you see and what you believe needs to be done. Do your homework first. Have documented support for the problems that tend to emerge from the current practice and several workable solutions to improve the situation. Do you have a colleague who is more informed about office politics? Could she advise you of the most effective way to proceed?

The change you wish to implement might start with nothing more than developing a voice among your colleagues. Don't minimize the importance of beginning within yourself by demanding the respect you deserve. Eeva Sallinen Simard encourages women to "*expect* to be counted."[16] How do you do that? By speaking up when you have a contribution to make. Are you interrupted? Make it clear that you were not finished speaking. Are your ideas credited to others? Don't dismiss it without talking to those who need to know.

I realize that some battles are more critical than others. Some companies require more changes than one person can make. And likeminded colleagues willing to go the distance with you might be scarce. Therefore, gauge the seriousness of the slights and whether they will exact a price in terms of career advancement, for yourself

[16]Simard, "Women at Work," 13.

or others. If you determine you can do no more, consider looking elsewhere for a place to fulfill your professional calling. Don't dismiss what you have to offer based on the inflexibility of one workplace.

Whether you are positioned to make sweeping changes or must take incremental steps, begin today moving toward your goal. Whatever you accomplish and in whatever time it takes, you will have helped create a culture of achievement based on ability and calling rather than gender.

Places you do business. Do not underestimate your power to effect change on a bigger scale than within your local institutions. When joined with others, your efforts can affect businesses that reach into national or worldwide markets. Such has been the case when a variety of retailers discontinued merchandise after customers complained. JCPenney discontinued a T-shirt marketed for girls ages seven to sixteen with the statement "I'm too pretty to do homework so my brother has to do it for me."[17] This removal came after an online petition asked for the shirt's removal from the company's website.[18] Abercrombie and Fitch's shirt boasting "With these, who needs brains" was pulled in response to complaints led by fewer than two dozen teenage girls from the Allegheny County Girls as Grantmakers group.[19] Mattel's Barbie doll stopped spouting "Math class is tough" after women of the American Association of University Women protested.[20] Objections to Forever 21's shirt

[17]"JCPenney's Girls Are Too Pretty for Homework T-shirt Sends Worst Message Ever [Update]," *Huffpost*, December 6, 2017, www.huffpost.com/entry/jcpenney-too-pretty-for-homework_n_943423.

[18]Allison Berry, "JCPenny Yanks 'I'm Too Pretty to Do Homework' T-shirt After Online Outcry," *Time*, September 1, 2011, https://newsfeed.time.com/2011/09/01/jcpenney-yanks-im-too-pretty-to-do-homework-t-shirt-after-online-outcry/.

[19]Brandee J. Tecson, "Abercrombie Pulls T-shirts After Teen Girls Launch Boycott," MTV News, November 7, 2005, www.mtv.com/news/1513153/abercrombie-pulls-t-shirts-after-teen-girls-launch-boycott/.

[20]"Company News: Mattel Says It Erred; Teen Talk Barbie Turns Silent on Math," *New York Times*, October 21, 1992, www.nytimes.com/1992/10/21/business/company-news-mattel-says-it-erred-teen-talk-barbie-turns-silent-on-math.html.

announcing "Allergic to Algebra" resulted in it also being taken off the shelves.[21] Gymboree's onesies for boys that brandished "Smart like Daddy" and those for girls saying "Pretty like Mommy" were removed in response to criticism.[22]

The bottom line for any business is the sale of its products. Nothing will motivate change like a drop in sales. When you see a product that diminishes women as achievers, consigning their interests to beauty and their abilities to getting a guy's attention, speak up. Communicate directly with companies that manufacture and sell such products. Let them know why it is offensive, that you demand change, and what you will do to make others aware. Ask others to join you in holding these companies accountable. Tell your friends. Tell the parents of your children's friends. Post the product on social media, stating why the message is harmful and whom to contact to register an objection. Encourage others to do the same. Your complaint combined with those of others can change what we see on store shelves and, in turn, what our culture consumes to the detriment of girls and women everywhere.

This chapter presents a few possibilities you can put into practice to solidify what you have learned throughout this book. Hopefully, you see that the opportunities for effecting change are limitless. Small adjustments in the way we think and behave often lead to bigger changes as we become more confident in our ability to make a difference. Some of the ideas suggested here will be easy to implement; others will be more difficult. I hope, however, that you will take the first steps in creating the change you wish to see in your

---

[21] Feifei Sun, "Forever 21 Pulls 'Allergic to Algebra' T-shirt After Critics Cry Foul," *Time*, September 13, 2011, https://newsfeed.time.com/2011/09/13/forever-21-pulls-allergic-to-algebra-t-shirt-after-critics-cry-foul/#:~:text=Just%20a%20couple%20weeks%20after,worst%20thing%20in%20the%20world.

[22] "Remove Onesie Messages: 'Smart Like Dad' and 'Pretty Like Mom,'" Change.org, www.change.org/p/gymboree-remove-onesie-messages-smart-like-dad-and-pretty-like-mom.

world and that your efforts will bolster your self-confidence and inspire others to join in the work.

RECOMMENDED READING

Cole, Kadi. *Developing Female Leaders: Navigate the Minefields and Release the Potential of Women in Your Church.* Nashville: Thomas Nelson, 2019.

Gates, Melinda. *The Moment of Lift: How Empowering Women Changes the World.* New York: Flatiron, 2019.

Krueger, Ron. "4 Bible Translation Basics Every Christian Should Know." *Mutuality Blog + Magazine.* December 4, 2017. www.cbeinternational.org/resource/article/mutuality-blog-magazine/4-bible-translation-basics-every-christian-should-know.

Lewis, Karoline M. *SHE: Five Keys to Unlock the Power of Women in Ministry.* Nashville: Abingdon, 2016.

Morgante, Camden. "When Religion Hurts: How Complementarian Churches Harm Women." CBE Blog/Magazine. May 19, 2021. www.cbeinternational.org/resource/article/mutuality-blog-magazine/when-religion-hurts-how-complementarian-churches-harm.

"Raising a Concern with Your Child's School." Let Toys Be Toys. www.lettoysbetoys.org.uk/resources/parents-raising-an-issue-with-your-childs-school/.

Richardson, Jill. "The Subtle Hazing of Women in Ministry." CBE Blog/Magazine. November 6, 2019. www.cbeinternational.org/resource/article/mutuality-blog-magazine/subtle-hazing-women-ministry.

Simard, Eeva Sallinen. "Women at Work: 3 Things I Wish I Knew When I Graduated College." *Mutuality Blog + Magazine.* September 4, 2019. www.cbeinternational.org/resource/article/mutuality-blog-magazine/women-work-3-things-i-wish-i-knew-when-i-graduated-college.

Wallace, Gail. "4 Reasons to Use a Gender-Accurate Bible Translation." *Mutuality Blog + Magazine.* December 4, 2017. www.cbeinternational.org/resource/article/mutuality-blog-magazine/4-reasons-use-gender-accurate-bible-translation.

EPILOGUE

"If God calls women to pastor, why don't more churches have women leaders?" This question from a student in my gender studies course prompted me to emphasize the power of implicit socialization in how we each respond to God's call. That emphasis now permeates my teaching and prompted the writing of this book. In fact, helping others identify and counter gendered socialization so they are freer to live more fully is an integral part of my own calling. As such, I hope this book has done that for you.

I hope that your eyes are now open to the messages you have received and the self-perceptions they have created. As you assess those perceptions for accuracy, I pray that you will let go of any not supported by the evidence and replace them with those based on truth so you will be freer to step into your own calling.

In her book *Liberating Tradition*, Kristina LaCelle-Peterson likens the use of our abilities to the servants' stewardship of their master's wealth in Matthew 25:14-27.[1] Each servant was given talents of gold for which they would be held accountable at the master's return. Those who "put [their] money to work" (Matthew 25:16) were able

[1]Kristina LaCelle-Peterson, *Liberating Tradition: Women's Identity and Vocation in Christian Perspective* (Grand Rapids, MI: Baker Academic, 2008), 113.

to present the master with an increase and on his return received his praise. The one who buried his talent, however, had no increase and received his master's rebuke. LaCelle-Peterson suggests that women who bury their talents will not get a pass. "Would the returning master of the household be mollified if the excuse for burying one's talent was, 'I got married,' or 'My husband didn't want me to'?"[2]

Indeed.

The world is changing as each generation moves us closer to redeeming the breach reflected in Genesis 3:16. And this redemption is something in which we can all participate. I hope the suggestions provided in the last chapter inspire you to make changes within your own world and within the culture at large.

One woman whose ministry has spanned church leadership and academia underscored the importance of working for change and the hope it brings. She recounted the obstacles she had faced throughout her formal education and beyond. In college she was told that a man should make her decisions. In seminary, her professors' consistent references to "the *man* of God" left her "devastated at being left out." While her male seminary friends were paid for their church work, she was not. Later, when applying for a promotion at the seminary where she was on faculty, her dean commented, "You don't look like a full professor."

Nonetheless, she expressed hope. She told me that once after preaching a sermon she saw two elementary-school girls playing church, taking turns being the preacher. The reality these girls had experienced was already quite different from the one she had experienced. She and others within their congregation were creating a new narrative for these girls and for the women they would become.

I hope that you too will lean into a world that encourages women and men alike to develop fully and to follow their call wherever it

---

[2]LaCelle-Peterson, *Liberating Tradition*, 113.

takes them. And I hope that like the woman who didn't "look like a full professor"—and regardless of any obstacles you've faced—you have hope. Just as we are all participants in the breach between the sexes, we are also called to be part of the redemption.

I find that inspiring. I hope you do too.

DISCUSSION GUIDE

1. What are your earliest memories of boys and girls receiving different treatment? What messages did you take away from those experiences?
2. What toys were you encouraged or discouraged from playing with as a child? How did that influence your interests or perception of your abilities?
3. How would you have completed the following sentence when you were very young? "When I grow up, I want to be a(n) . . ." If you remember telling that to anyone, how did they respond? What messages did you get from their reactions?
4. When choosing an occupation, did you see it as contributing to or detracting from your (future) family's quality of life? Did you assume that you or your partner would be caring for (future) children? How did these assumptions influence your occupational decisions?
5. What chores were you assigned as a child or teen? What skills and mindset did they help you develop?
6. If you went to church growing up, what roles did men and women fill there? What did that communicate to you about your future role within the church?

7. What were your favorite subjects in elementary school? In which did you feel most competent? Did that change as you reached high school? If so, why?
8. What attributions did you, your parents, and teachers make for your success or failure in different school subjects?
9. Who were your heroes as a child? Were they the same sex as you? Did you see yourself accomplishing things they did?
10. Select a sexist word or phrase you have found yourself using. Be intentional this week about replacing it with a nonsexist alternative. Did the change modify your gendered perceptions?
11. Make a list of twenty words or phrases that describe who you are. (Don't move on to the rest of this question until you've made your list.)

    Now, look at your list of descriptors. Do they identify characteristics of yourself as an individual (e.g., musician, avid reader, intelligent) or the roles you fill for others (mother, friend, employee)? While both certainly have value, an identity that encompasses both might be a good balance. Go back to your list and for every role statement, add one that emphasizes your individuality and vice versa. Does that broaden your self-perception?
12. The next time you voice something you want or need, notice your choice of words. Is your speech direct, or do you hedge? Ask an objective, trustworthy person if you sounded confident and committed to attaining what you asked for. If their assessment reveals that you did not, practice communicating what you want with confidence and commitment. How does the rephrase feel to you? Which method of communication is more likely to result in a satisfying outcome?

13. What have you learned about yourself from this book? In what ways has the information presented here reflected your own experience? Where has your experience differed?
14. Are there changes you would like to make? If so, which of the suggested techniques would help you achieve this change? What obstacles do you foresee? How might you overcome those obstacles?
15. Identify parts of your support system that will help you reach your goals. How could you strengthen your support system?
16. Identify a micro- and macrolevel action you could employ to help you begin changing your world and solidify changes you've made within yourself. Which one can you implement this week?

RESOURCES FOR WOMEN'S NETWORKING

American Association of University Women. www.aauw.org.

American Medical Women's Association. www.amwa-doc.org.

Association for Women in Mathematics. https://awm-math.org.

Association for Women in Science. www.awis.org.

Biblical Christian Egalitarians. www.facebook.com/groups/BiblicalChristian Egalitarians/.

Christians for Biblical Equality. www.cbeinternational.org.

Financial Women's Association. www.fwa.org.

Girls Inc. https://girlsinc.org/about-us/.

International Association of Women. https://careers.iawomen.com.

International Association of Women Ministers. http://womenministers.org/site /welcome.

International Federation of Business and Professional Women. www.bpw -international.org.

Institute for Biblical Research—IBR Women. https://ibr-bbr.org/about/ibr-women.

InterVarsity Women in the Academy and Professions. https://thewell.intervarsity.org/.

National Association of Women in Construction. www.nawic.org/nawic/default.asp.

National Organization for Women. https://now.org.

Society for Women Engineers. https://swe.org/.

Women in Film and Television International. www.wifti.net.

Women in Technology International. https://witi.com.

Women's Caucus for Art. https://nationalwca.org.

BIBLIOGRAPHY

Acciai, Francesco, and Melissa Hardy. "Depression in Later Life: A Closer Look at the Gender Gap." *Social Science Research* 68 (2017): 163-75.

American Psychological Association. Report of the APA Task Force on the Sexualization of Girls. 2007. www.apa.org/pi/women/programs/girls/report-full.pdf.

Androutsopoulou, Athena, and Maria Viou. "The Guided Imagery Therapy Activity 'Inner Dialogue-Child Adult Meeting' (ID-CAM): Steps and Applications." *Journal of Creativity in Mental Health* 14, no. 3 (2019): 343-56.

Bell, Lee Anne. "In Danger of Winning: Consciousness Raising Strategies for Empowering Girls in the United States." *Women's Studies International Forum* 19, no. 4 (1996): 419-27.

Berry, Allison. "JCPenny Yanks 'I'm Too Pretty to Do Homework' T-Shirt After Online Outcry." *Time*. September 1, 2011. https://newsfeed.time.com/2011/09/01/jcpenney-yanks-im-too-pretty-to-do-homework-t-shirt-after-online-outcry/.

Blair, Irene V., Jennifer E. Ma, and Alison P. Lenton. "Imagining Stereotypes Away: The Moderation of Implicit Stereotypes Through Mental Imagery." *Journal of Personality and Social Psychology* 81, no. 5 (2001): 828-41.

Blair-Loy, Mary, Arlie Hochschild, Allison J. Pugh, Joan C. Williams, and Heidi Hartmann. "Stability and Transformation in Gender, Work, and Family: Insights from *The Second Shift* for the Next Quarter Century." *Community, Work, and Family* 18, no. 4 (2015): 435-54.

Carlana, Michela. "Implicit Stereotypes: Evidence from Teachers' Gender Bias." *The Quarterly Journal of Economics* 134, no. 3 (2019): 1163-1224.

Chambless, Dianne. L., and Martha M. Gillis. "Cognitive Therapy of Anxiety Disorders." *Journal of Consulting and Clinical Psychology* 61, no. 2 (1993): 248-60.

Cho, S., M. Goodman, B. Oppenheimer, J. Codling, and T. Robinson. "Images of Women in STEM Fields." *Journal of Science Communication* 8, no. 3 (2009): 1-5.

Claro, Susana, David Paunesku, and Carol S. Dweck. "Growth Mindset Tempers the Effects of Poverty on Academic Achievement." *Proceedings of the National Academy of Sciences of the United States of America* 113, no. 31 (2016): 8664-68.

Cole, Kadi. *Developing Female Leaders.* Nashville: Thomas Nelson, 2019.

Collins, Suzanne. *The Hunger Games.* New York: Scholastic Press, 2008–2010.

"Company News: Mattel Says It Erred; Teen Talk Barbie Turns Silent on Math." *New York Times.* October 21, 1992. www.nytimes.com/1992/10/21/business/company-news-mattel-says-it-erred-teen-talk-barbie-turns-silent-on-math.html.

Cooper, Shauna, M. "Associations Between Father-Daughter Relationship Quality and the Academic Engagement of African American Adolescent Girls: Self-Esteem as a Mediator?" *Journal of Black Psychology* 35, no. 4 (2009): 495-516.

Croft, Alyssa, Toni Schmader, Katharina Block, and Andrew Scott Baron. "The Second Shift Reflected in the Second Generation: Do Parents' Gender Roles at Home Predict Children's Aspirations?" *Psychological Science* 25, no. 7 (2014): 1418-28.

Crombie, Gail, Nancy Sinclair, Naida Silverthorn, Barbara M. Byrne, David L. DuBois, and Anne Trinneer. "Predictors of Young Adolescents' Math Grades and Course Enrollment Intentions: Gender Similarities and Differences." *Sex Roles* 52, nos. 5/6 (2005): 351-67.

Crowley, Kevin, Maureen A. Callanan, Harriet R. Tenenbaum, and Elizabeth Allen. "Parents Explain More Often to Boys Than to Girls During Shared Scientific Thinking." *Psychological Science* 12, no. 3 (2001): 258-61.

Daubman, Kimberly A., and Harold Sigall. "Gender Differences in Perceptions of How Others Are Affected by Self-Disclosure of Achievement." *Sex Roles* 37, no. 1/2 (1997): 73-89.

Dickhauser, Oliver, and Wulf-Uwe Meyer. "Gender Differences in Young Children's Math Ability Attributions." *Psychology Science* 48, no. 1 (2006): 3-16.

Digest of Education Statistics. "Bachelor's Degrees Conferred to Females by Postsecondary Institutions, by Race/Ethnicity and Field of Study: 2017–2018 and 2018–2019." National Center for Education Statistics. https://nces.ed.gov/programs/digest/d20/tables/dt20_322.50.asp.

Digest of Education Statistics. "Bachelor's Degrees Conferred to Males by Postsecondary Institutions, by Race/Ethnicity and Field of Study: 2017–2018 and 2018–2019." National Center for Education Statistics. https://nces.ed.gov/programs/digest/d20/tables/dt20_322.40.asp.

Digest of Education Statistics. "Recent High School Completers and Their Enrollment in College, by Sex and Level of Institution: 1960–2019." National Center for Education Statistics. https://nces.ed.gov/programs/digest/d20/tables/dt20_302.10.asp.

Dobson, Keith S. "A Meta-Analysis of the Efficacy of Cognitive Therapy for Depression." *Journal of Consulting and Clinical Psychology* 57 (1989): 414-19.

Dumont, Eric, Anita Jansen, Diana Kroes, Eline de Haan, and Sandra Mulkens. "A New Cognitive Behavior Therapy for Adolescents with Avoidant/Restrictive Food

Intake Disorder in a Day Treatment Setting: A Clinical Case Series." *International Journal of Eating Disorders* 52 (2019): 447-58.

Eagly, Alice H., and Seven J. Karau. "Role Congruity Theory of Prejudice Toward Female Leaders." *Psychological Review* 109, no. 3 (2002): 573-98.

Else-Quest, Nicole M., Janet Shibley Hyde, and Marcia C. Linn. "Cross-National Patterns of Gender Differences in Mathematics: A Meta-Analysis." *Psychological Bulletin* 136, no. 1 (2010): 103-27.

Erikson, Erik H. *The Life Cycle Completed: A Review*. New York: W. W. Norton, 1982.

———. *Identity: Youth and Crisis*. New York: W. W. Norton & Company, 1968.

Faber, Frederick William. *Faith of Our Fathers*, 1849.

Fine, Cordelia, and Emma Rush. "'Why Does All the Girls Have to Buy Pink Stuff?' The Ethics and Science of the Gendered Toy Marketing Debate." *Journal of Business Ethics* 149 (2018): 769-84.

Frome, Pamela M., Corinne J. Alfeld, Jacquelynne S. Eccles, and Bonnie L. Barber. "Why Don't They Want a Male-Dominated Job? An Investigation of Young Women Who Changed Their Occupational Aspirations." *Educational Research and Evaluation* 12, no. 4 (2006): 359-72.

Georgakaki, Styliani Kyriaki, and Eirini Karakasidou. "The Effects of Motivational Self-Talk on Competitive Anxiety and Self-Compassion: A Brief Training Program Among Competitive Swimmers." *Scientific Research Publishing* 8, no. 5 (2017): 677-99.

Gilligan, Carol. *In a Different Voice: Psychological Theory and Women's Development*. Cambridge, MA: Harvard University Press, 1993.

Glass, Jennifer L., Sharon Sassler, Yael Levitte, and Katherine M. Michelmore. "What's So Special About STEM? A Comparison of Women's Retention in STEM and Professional Occupations." *Social Forces* 92, no. 2 (2013): 723-56.

Gloaguen, Valerie, Jean Cottraux, Michel Cucherat, and Ivy-Marie Blackburn. "A Meta-Analysis of the Effects of Cognitive Therapy in Depressed Patients." *Journal of Affective Disorders* 49 (1998): 59-72.

Gooding, Gretchen E., and Rose M. Kreider. "Women's Marital Naming Choices in a Nationally Representative Sample." *Journal of Family Issues* 31, no. 5 (2010): 681-701.

Heatherington, Laurie, Kimberly A. Daubman, Cynthia Bates, Alicia Ahn, Heather Brown, and Camille Preston. "Two Investigations of 'Female Modesty' in Achievement Situations." *Sex Roles* 29, no. 11/12 (1993): 739-54.

Heaverlo, Carol A., Robyn Cooper, and Frankie Santos Lannan. "STEM Development: Predictors for 6th-12th Grade Girls' Interest and Confidence in Science and Math." *Journal of Women and Minorities in Science and Engineering* 19, no. 2 (2013): 121-42.

Heilman, Madeline E., Aaron S. Wallen, Daniella Fuchs, and Melinda M. Tamkins. "Penalties for Success: Reactions to Women Who Succeed at Male Gender-Typed Tasks." *Journal of Applied Psychology* 89, no. 3 (2004): 416-27.

Herbert, Jennifer, and Deborah Stipek. "The Emergence of Gender Differences in Children's Perceptions of Their Academic Competence." *Journal of Applied Developmental Psychology* 26 (2005): 276-95.

Hestbech, Asser Mikkel. "Reclaiming the Inner Child in Cognitive-Behavioral Therapy: The Complementary Model of the Personality." *American Journal of Psychotherapy* 71, no. 1 (2018): 21-27.

Hiebert, Frances. "Beginning at the Beginning." *Priscilla Papers* 3, no. 3 (1989): 13-16. www.cbeinternational.org/resource/article/priscilla-papers-academic-journal/beginning-beginning.

Hochschild, Arlie, with Anne Machung. *The Second Shift: Working Families and the Revolution at Home*. New York: Penguin, 1989.

Honyashiki, Mina, Toshi A. Furukawa, Hisashi Noma, Shiro Tanaka, Peiyao Chen, Kayoko Ichikawa, Miki Ono, Rachel Churchill, Vivien Hunot, and Deborah M. Caldwell. "Specificity of CBT for Depression: A Contribution from Multiple Treatments Meta-analyses." *Cognitive Therapy Research* 38 (2014): 249-60.

Horner, Matina S. "Toward an Understanding of Achievement-Related Conflicts in Women." *Journal of Social Issues* 28, no. 2 (1972): 157-75.

Hyde, Janet S., Sara M. Lindberg, Marcia C. Linn, Amy B. Ellis, and Caroline C. Williams. "Gender Similarities Characterize Math Performance." *Science* 321, no. 5888 (2008): 494-95.

Jaffee, Sara, and Janet Shibley Hyde. "Gender Differences in Moral Orientation: A Meta-analysis." *Psychological Bulletin* 126, no. 5 (2000): 703-26.

"JCPenney's Girls Are Too Pretty for Homework T-Shirt Sends Worst Message Ever [Update]." *Huffpost*. December 6, 2017. www.huffpost.com/entry/jcpenney-too-pretty-for-homework_n_943423.

Johnson, J. J. *Dino Dana*. Culver City, CA: Amazon Studios in Association with Sinking Ship Entertainment, 2017–present.

Kay, Eve. "Call Me Ms." *The Guardian*. June 29, 2007. www.theguardian.com/world/2007/jun/29/gender.uk.

Keles, Serap, and Thormod Idsoe. "A Meta-Analysis of Group Cognitive-Behavioral Therapy (CBT) Interventions for Adolescents with Depression." *Journal of Adolescence* 67 (2018): 129-39.

Khattab, Jasmien, and Hannes Leroy. "An Authenticity Approach to Role Congruity Theory." *Proceedings of Academy of Management Annual Meeting*. November 30, 2017.

Koburtay, Tamer, Jawad Syed, and Radi Haloub. "Congruity Between the Female Gender Role and the Leader Role: A Literature Review." *European Business Review* 31, no. 6 (2019): 831-48.

Koch, Amanda J., Susan D. D'Mello, and Paul R. Sackett. "A Meta-Analysis of Gender Stereotypes and Bias in Experimental Simulations of Employment Decision Making." *Journal of Applied Psychology* 100, no. 1 (2015): 128-61.

Kohlberg, Lawrence. *Essays on Moral Development*. Vol. 1, *The Philosophy of Moral Development: Moral Stages and the Idea of Justice*. San Francisco: Harper & Row, 1981.

Kubu, Cynthia S. "Who Does She Think She Is? Women, Leadership and the 'B'(ias) Word." *The Clinical Neuropsychologist* 32, no. 2 (2018): 235-51.

LaCelle-Peterson, Kristina. *Liberating Tradition: Women's Identity and Vocation in Christian Perspective*. Grand Rapids, MI: Baker Academic, 2008.

Lachance-Grzela, Mylene, and Genevieve Bouchard. "Why Do Women Do the Lion's Share of Housework? A Decade of Research." *Sex Roles* 63 (2010): 767-80.

Lavy, Victor, and Edith Sand. "On the Origins of Gender Gaps in Human Capital: Short- and Long-Term Consequences of Teachers' Biases." *Journal of Public Economics* 167 (2018): 263-79.

Lind, Georg. "Measuring Moral Judgment: A Review of *The Measurement of Moral Judgment* by Anne Colby and Lawrence Kohlberg." *Human Development* 32 (1989): 388-97.

Livingston, Robert W., Ashleigh Shelby Rosette, and Ella F. Washington. "Can an Agentic Black Woman Get Ahead? The Impact of Race and Interpersonal Dominance on Perceptions of Female Leaders." *Psychological Science* 23, no. 4 (2012): 354-58.

Maji, Sucharita. "Society and 'Good Woman': A Critical Review of Gender Difference in Depression." *International Journal of Social Psychiatry*. March 30, 2018.

Marigold, Denise C., John G. Holmes, and Michael Ross. "More Than Words: Reframing Compliments from Romantic Partners Fosters Security in Low Self-Esteem Individuals." *Journal of Personality and Social Psychology* 92, no. 2 (2007): 232-48.

Marks, Gillian, and Diane M. Houston. "The Determinants of Young Women's Intentions About Education, Career Development and Family Life." *Journal of Education and Work* 15, no. 3 (2002): 321-36.

Matteson, David R. "Differences Within and Between Genders: A Challenge to the Theory." In *Ego Identity: A Handbook for Psychosocial Research*, edited by J. E. Marcia, A. S. Waterman, D. R. Matteson, S.L. Archer, and J. L. Orlofsky, 69-441. New York: Springer-Verlag, 1993.

Mau, Wei-Cheng. "Factors That Influence Persistence in Science and Engineering Career Aspirations." *The Career Development Quarterly* 51 (2003): 234-43.

McCracken, Craig. *Powerpuff Girls*. Burbank, CA: Cartoon Network Studios, 1998–2005.

Merrill, William P. *Rise Up, O Men of God*. 1911.

Mulac, Anthony. "The Gender-Linked Language Effect: Do Language Differences Really Make a Difference?" In *Sex Differences and Similarities in Communication*, edited by Daniel J. Canary and Kathryn Dindia, 219-39. 2nd ed. New York: Routledge, 2006.

Myer, David G., and Malcolm A. Jeeves. *Psychology Through the Eyes of Faith*. Rev. ed. New York: HarperCollins, 2003.

Nee, Chris. *Doc McStuffins*. Dublin, Ireland: Brown Bag Films, 2015–2020.

Nunberg, Geoff. "Everyone Uses Singular 'They,' Whether They Realize It or Not." *Fresh Air*. NPR. January 13, 2016. www.npr.org/2016/01/13/462906419/everyone-uses-singular-they-whether-they-realize-it-or-not.

O'Brien, Karen M., Suzanne Miller Friedman, Linda C. Tipton, and Sonja Geschmay Linn. "Attachment, Separation, and Women's Vocational Development: A Longitudinal Analysis." *Journal of Counseling Psychology* 47, no. 3 (2000): 301-15.

Ochman, Jan M. "The Effects of Nongender-Role Stereotyped, Same-Sex Role Models in Storybooks on the Self-Esteem of Children in Grade Three." *Sex Roles* 35, no. 11-12 (1996): 711-35.

Olivo, Christiane. "Bringing Women In: Gender and American Government and Politics Textbooks." *Journal of Political Science Education* 8 (2012): 131-46.

Oppliger, Patrice. "Effects of Gender Stereotyping on Socialization." In *Mass Media Effects Research: Advances Through Meta-Analysis*, edited by Raymond W. Preiss, Barbara Mae Gayle, Nancy Burrell, Mike Allen, and Jennings Bryant, 199-214. Mahwah, NJ: Lawrence Erlbaum Associates, 2007.

Pesut, Daniel J. "The Art, Science, and Techniques of Reframing in Psychiatric Mental Health Nursing." *Issues in Mental Health Nursing* 12, no. 1 (1991): 9-18.

"Raising a Concern with Your Child's School." Let Toys Be Toys. www.lettoysbetoys.org.uk/resources/parents-raising-an-issue-with-your-childs-school/.

Raley, Sara, and Suzanne Bianchi. "Sons, Daughters, and Family Processes: Does Gender of Children Matter?" *Annual Review of Sociology* 32 (2006): 401-21.

Ratliff, Kate A., and Shigehiro Oishi. "Gender Differences in Implicit Self-Esteem Following a Romantic Partner's Success or Failure." *Journal of Personality and Social Psychology* 105, no. 4 (2013): 688-702.

Raty, Hannu, Johanna Vanska, Kati Kasanen, and Riitta Karkkainen. "Parents' Explanations of Their Child's Performance in Mathematics and Reading: A Replication and Extension of Yee and Eccles." *Sex Roles* 46, no. 3/4 (2002): 121-28.

"Remove Onesie Messages: 'Smart Like Dad' and 'Pretty Like Mom.'" Change.org. www.change.org/p/gymboree-remove-onesie-messages-smart-like-dad-and-pretty-like-mom.

Richardson, Jill. "The Subtle Hazing of Women in Ministry." Christians for Biblical Equality. November 6, 2019. www.cbeinternational.org/resource/article/mutuality-blog-magazine/subtle-hazing-women-ministry.

Riecher-Rossler, Anita. "Sex and Gender Differences in Mental Disorders." *The Lancet* 4 (2017): www.thelancet.com/journals/lanpsy/article/PIIS2215-0366(16)30348-0/fulltext.

Roberts, Laura R., and Anne C. Petersen. "The Relationship Between Academic Achievement and Social Self-Image During Early Adolescence." *Journal of Early Adolescence 12*, no. 2 (1992): 197-219.

Robinson-Cimpian, Joseph P., Sarah Theule Lubienski, Colleen M. Ganley, and Yasemin Copur-Gencturk. "Teachers' Perceptions of Students' Mathematics Proficiency May Exacerbate Early Gender Gaps in Achievement." *Developmental Psychology* 50, no. 4 (2014): 1262-81.

Rosino, Michael, "ABC-X Model of Family Stress and Coping." In *The Wiley Blackwell Encyclopedia of Family Studies*, edited by Constance L. Shehan. New York: John Wiley & Sons, 2016.

Roth, Veronica. *Divergent*. New York: HarperCollins, 2011–2013.

Rowling, J. K. *Harry Potter*. New York: Arthur A. Levine, 1997–2016.

Salk, R. H., J. S. Hyde, and L. Y. Abramson. "Gender Differences in Depression in Representative National Samples: Meta-Analyses of Diagnoses and Symptoms." *Psychological Bulletin* 143, no. 8 (2017): 783-822.

Schock, Anne-Kathrin, Freya M. Gruber, Thomas Scherndl, and Tuulia M. Ortner. "Tempering Agency with Communion Increases Women's Leadership Emergence in All-Women Groups: Evidence for Role Congruity Theory in a Field Setting." *The Leadership Quarterly* 30 (2019): 189-98.

Schwalbe, Michael L., and Clifford L. Staples. "Gender Differences in Sources of Self-Esteem." *Social Psychology Quarterly* 54, no. 2 (1991): 158-68.

Seedat, Soraya et al. "Cross-National Associations Between Gender and Mental Disorders in the World Health Organization World Mental Health Surveys." *Arch Gen Psychiatry* 66, no. 7 (2009): 785-95.

Shi, Xiaowei, Thomas M. Brinthaupt, and Margaret McCree. "The Relationship of Self-Talk Frequency to Communication Apprehension and Public Speaking Anxiety." *Personality and Individual Differences* 75 (2015): 125-29.

Shurer, Osnat. *Moana*. Burbank, CA: Walt Disney Animation Studios, 2016.

Siev, Jedidiah, and Dianne L. Chambless. "Specificity of Treatment Effects: Cognitive Therapy and Relaxation for Generalized Anxiety and Panic Disorders." *Journal of Consulting and Clinical Psychology* 75, no. 4 (2007): 513-22.

Simard, Eeva Sallinen. "Women at Work: 3 Things I Wish I Knew When I Graduated College." *Mutuality* (2019): 11-15.

Sjoblom, Margareta, Lars Jacobsson, Kerstin Ohrling, and Catrine Kostenius. "From 9 to 91: Health Promotion Through the Life-Course—Illuminating the Inner Child." *Health Promotion International* (2020): 1-10.

Smith, Jeffery. *Psychotherapy: A Practical Guide*. New York: Springer, 2017.

Steinhilber, Kylie M., Sukanya Ray, Debra A. Harkins, and Megan E. Sienkiewicz. "Father-Daughter Relationship Dynamics and Daughters' Body Image, Eating Patterns, and Empowerment: An Exploratory Study." *Women and Health* 60, no. 10 (2020): 1083-94.

Steffens, Melanie C., Petra Jelenec, and Peter Noack. "On the Leaky Math Pipeline: Comparing Implicit Math-Gender Stereotypes and Math Withdrawal in Female and Male Children and Adolescents." *Journal of Educational Psychology* 102, no. 4 (2010): 947-63.

Sun, Feifei. "Forever 21 Pulls 'Allergic to Algebra' T-Shirt After Critics Cry Foul." *Time*. September 13, 2011. https://newsfeed.time.com/2011/09/13/forever-21-pulls-allergic-to-algebra-t-shirt-after-critics-cry-foul/.

Tecson, Brandee J. "Abercrombie Pulls T-Shirts After Teen Girls Launch Boycott." *MTV News*. November 7, 2005. www.mtv.com/news/1513153/abercrombie-pulls-t-shirts-after-teen-girls-launch-boycott/.

Tenenbaum, Harriet R., and Dionna May. "Gender in Parent-Child Relationships." In *Gender and Development*, edited by Patrick J. Leman and Harriet R. Tenenbaum, 1-19. London: Psychology Press, 2014.

Thomaes, Sander, Iris Charlotte Tjaarda, Eddie Brummelman, and Constantine Sedikides. "Effort Self-Talk Benefits the Mathematics Performance of Children with Negative Competence Beliefs." *Child Development* 91, no. 6 (2019): 2211-20.

Todd, Brenda K., Rico A. Fischer, Steven Di Costa, Amanda Roestorf, Kate Harbour, Paul Hardiman, and John A. Barry. "Sex Differences in Children's Toy Preferences: A Systematic Review, Meta-Regression, and Meta-Analysis." *Infant and Child Development* 27, no. 2 (2018).

Twenge, Jean M., and Susan Nolen-Hoeksema. "Age, Gender, Race, Socioeconomic Status, and Birth Cohort Differences on the Children's Depression Inventory: A Meta-Analysis." *Journal of Abnormal Psychology* 111, no. 4 (2002): 578-88.

Van Straten, Annemieke, Tanja van der Zweerde, Annet Kleiboer, Pim Cuijpers, Charles M. Morin, and Jaap Lancee. "Cognitive and Behavioral Therapies in the Treatment of Insomnia: A Meta-Analysis." *Sleep Medicine Reviews* 38 (2018): 3-16.

Van Willigen, Marieke, and Patricia Drentea. "Benefits of Equitable Relationships: The Impact of Sense of Fairness, Household Division of Labor, and Decision Making Power on Perceived Social Support." *Sex Roles* 44, no. 9/10 (2001): 571-97.

Vancampfort, Davy, Michel Probst, An Adriaens, Guido Pieters, Marc De Hert, Brendon Stubbs, Andy Soundy, and Johan Vanderlinden. "Changes in Physical Activity, Physical Fitness, Self-Perception and Quality of Life Following a 6-Month Physical Activity Counseling and Cognitive Behavioral Therapy Program in Outpatients with Binge Eating Disorder." *Psychiatry Research* 219, no. 2 (2014): 361-66.

Viljaranta, Jaana, Gintautas Silinskas, Marja-Kristiina Lerkkanen, Riikka Hirvonen, Eija Pakarinen, Anna-Maija Poikkeus, and Jari-Erik Nurmi. "Maternal Homework Assistance and Children's Task-Persistent Behavior in Elementary School." *Learning and Instruction* 56 (2018): 54-63.

Wallington, Aury. *Spirit Riding Free*. Glendale, CA: DreamWorks Animation Television, 2017–2019.

Watts, Sarah E., Adrienne Turnell, Natalie Kladnitski, Jill M. Newby, and Gavin Andrews. "Treatment-as-Usual (TAU) Is Anything but Usual: A Meta-Analysis of CBT Versus TAU for Anxiety and Depression." *Journal of Affective Disorders* 175 (2015): 152-67.

Weiner, Eric, Chris Gifford, and Valerie Walsh. *Dora the Explorer*. Burbank, CA: Nickelodeon Studios, 2000–2019.

Whisenant, Warren, Debbiesiu L. Lee, and Windy Dees. "Role Congruity Theory: Perceptions of Fairness and Sexism in Sport Management." *Public Organization Review* 15 (2015): 475-85.

Worthington, Everett L., Jr. *Forgiveness and Reconciliation: Theory and Application.* New York: Routledge, 2006.

Zia, Asbah, Anila Amber Malik, and Saima Masoom Ali. "Father and Daughter Relationship and Its Impact on Daughter's Self-Esteem and Academic Achievement." *Academic Journal of Interdisciplinary Studies* 4, no. 1 (2015): 311-16.

Zurbriggen, Eileen L., and Elizabeth M. Morgan. "Who Wants to Marry a Millionaire? Reality Dating Television Programs, Attitudes Toward Sex, and Sexual Behaviors." *Sex Roles* 54, no. 1/2 (2006): 1-17.